Psychosynthesis in Education

Psychosynthesis provides a deep understanding of human development and potential. This book shows its value in the field of education and includes practical techniques and exercises for working with young people.

FOR JASON

Psychosynthesis in Education

A Guide to the Joy of Learning

by

DIANA WHITMORE
Foreword by Laura Huxley

TURNSTONE PRESS LIMITED
Wellingborough, Northamptonshire

8580

First published 1986

© DIANA WHITMORE 1986

British Library Cataloguing in Publication Data

Whitmore, Diana
   Psychosynthesis in Education
   1. Educational psychology
   I. Title
   370.15   LB1051

   ISBN 0-85500-223-9

Turnstone Press is part of the Thorsons Publishing Group

Printed and bound in Great Britain by
Anchor Brendon Ltd, Tiptree, Essex

CONTENTS

ACKNOWLEDGEMENTS

Roberto Assagioli was a student of Freud and a contemporary of Jung. He pioneered psychoanalysis in Italy but quickly saw its limitations. It did not encompass or embrace the higher aspects of man—creativity, inspiration, spiritual understanding and higher values like love, compassion, joy and wisdom—nor did it give recognition to man's existential search for meaning: a search which Assagioli believed to be an urge in human nature as basic and organic as any instinct or biological drive. As early as 1910 Assagioli began to formulate a holistic theory of man, encompassing the groundwork of Freud but also reaching for the stars.

Eloquent theories and models of the unfoldment of man require the addition of aliveness to portray fully the reality of life. This aliveness is often called the essence or spirit of such teachings. Assagioli was a human being who fully embodied the spirit or soul of his own teachings.

Who was this man? I asked myself before my visit to the *old sage* in Florence. And what was this spirit? It was not the important models, nor their useful application, that drew me to Italy for, coming from a broad and sophisticated background in the *human potential movement,* I was typically self-contained and all-knowing. However, I intuitively felt that this man had a unique quality and I was not to be disappointed.

The twilight of his life was gentle, serene and rich with grace. Through his guidance during our time together I was able to free myself of the self-imposed bondage of insecurities and fears—my spirit sparked into action—many negative areas seemed to melt away and were replaced with a vision of hope and promise for humanity and for myself. I deeply thank Roberto for this gift and for his inspiration, which persists as strongly now as it did during the last months of his life that I shared with him a decade ago.

Rather than being a closed system, psychosynthesis offers the opportunity for infinite diversity. Instead of handing down a finished product to his students, Assagioli offered them his vision and the chance to explore or create a large number of new avenues and methods. For this reason, many of the exercises which have been circulating in the international psychosynthesis community have gone through successive versions and variations. Identifying and acknowledging their originators would be impossible, therefore I thank the psychosynthesis community as a whole and acknowledge that many of the techniques and exercises that I use in this book are drawn from the conjointed effort of many people. In particular, I would like to recognize the fundamental contribution of the team of the San Francisco Psychosynthesis Institute for the inspiration and material it offered during the years 1973 to 1976.

I could not have begun to write this book without the support of the professionals: the psychosynthesis educators who have put in years of work in the classroom, bringing to life what I express here in words—Anita Courtman, Marilyn Feldberg, Lynn Gibson, Char Agostini and Mike Littledyke. Margo Russell and Hannah Blacher also gave me great help with the exercises, with feedback and with moral support. Over the years many students have provided me with the opportunity to teach and my debt to each of them is unquestionable.

I offer deep personal thanks to Richard Price and George Brown (who initiated the idea of this book), for their unshakable faith in my potential and for their tireless education of me; to Piero Ferrucci for his trust in me, his persistent collaboration over many years and his ceaseless demonstration of the principles of psychosynthesis; to John Whitmore for his patience and support throughout but especially with the task of editing; to Ann Huntley for the task of caring for my child and for loving him, while I wrote about children.

Finally, I thank you my little son Jason whose existence of three short years has done much the same for me as my experience with *old man* Assagioli. You have greatly reinforced my faith and trust in the essential goodness in all children and taught me reverence for the unspoiled beauty of the young.

FOREWORD

Parents and educators will undoubtedly welcome, cherish and make good use of Diana Whitmore's *Psychosynthesis in Education*. They deserve the respect and clarification that it gives them.

The needs of the young are no different than they were two or three generations ago, yet what a different world children find today! Where are the ever-forgiving grandparents, the adoring aunts and uncles, and the playful cousins, each giving their own kind of affection and education? Mobile society, changing marriage partners, intense materialism, and that ever-present intruder, the magic tube—potentially a marvellous tool but mostly a distributor of vulgarity and violence—these and other facts create an environment in which raising an emotionally secure child is unprecedentedly difficult. Coping with, and learning from, undue stress is a part of adult living—but for many children it comes much too soon.

Diana Whitmore's direct experience with children and adolescents, combined with her thorough knowledge of Psychosynthesis, has provided her with an unusual understanding of these problems and of how to work with them.

The exercises in this book capture our attention and imagination, while pointing to the power of inner-directed conscious will. The educator, acting as guide, does not need a specific academic background and will profit as much from the exercises as will the guided. They will deepen and clarify relationships in a graceful and pleasurable way.

All of us will do well to take note of the last chapter, for it makes us aware that the key to a better world for ourselves and our children does not lie in bigger and better tangibles: it lies within ourselves. This book is an answer to my *Prayer of the Unborn:*

> Men and Women who are on Earth
> You are our creators.
> We, the unborn, beseech you:
> Let us have living bread
> The builder of our new body.
> Let us have pure water
> The vitalizer of our blood.
> Let us have clean air
> So that every breath is a caress.
> Let us feel the petals of jasmine and roses
> Which are as tender as our skin.
>
> Men and women who are on Earth
> You are our creators.
> We, the unborn, beseech you:
> Do not give us a world of rage and fear
> For our minds will be rage and fear.
> Do not give us violence and pollution
> For our bodies will be disease and abomination.
>
> Let us be where ever we are
> Rather than bringing us
> Into a tormented self-destroying humanity.
>
> Men and women who are on Earth
> You are our creators.
> We, the unborn beseech you:
> If you are ready to love and be loved,
> Invite us to this Earth
> Of the Thousand Wonders,
> And we will be born
> To love and to be loved.

'I have written this book from my heart' states Diana Whitmore. May I add that she has written it from 'the heart that watches and receives'.

LAURA HUXLEY
July 1985—Los Angeles, California

INTRODUCTION

Imagine a child who perceives the world as a wonderfully exciting life-affirming place and who experiences adults as welcoming, guiding and supportive — as his* best friends. Imagine a child who feels appreciated; who feels worthwhile simply because he exists. Such a child would soon discover the wonder of life, the joy of exploring and learning and the beauty of understanding.

Imagine a child being encouraged to live each new awakening as a creative step in his unfoldment, as a wondrous opening to the fascinating world in which he finds himself. Imagine his response to the unknown being positive, full of curiosity and excitement. Imagine the brightly lit young eyes of children striving to conquer a difficult problem. Imagine children always being willing to reach out to help a fellow classmate.

Is this a 'Pollyanna' vision of how life might be for young people in an ideal world? Is it just the mystical dream of an eternal optimist? Is our responsibility as parents and educators limited to giving a child merely the practical tools to cope with life on a seemingly confused planet? Can we only educate them to *get by*? I do not think so. We have a responsibility, a heartfelt duty, to offer a vision for the future which includes both a realistic perception and assessment of troubled times, and an awareness of the incredible poignancy of life. Even if

*Throughout this book I am using masculine gender expressions in order to avoid the awkwardness of he/she or his/her.

our vision is only partially attainable it suggests great possibilities for holistic education.

There is little disagreement that the world today is facing extraordinary social stresses. Young people in particular are feeling increasingly ill-equipped to deal with domestic, social and international crises. They are confronted with problems which range from family conflicts, parental divorce, the breakdown of the nuclear family and their relationship with the adult world, to unemployment, environmental pollution and the threat of nuclear holocaust. Feelings of despair, meaninglessness and impotence accumulate with each problem a young person has to face. For adolescents these things are immediate concrete concerns, whereas younger children experience them in more indirect and confused ways, though no less painful ones. They can develop deep fears and unhealthy fantasies.

We should be greatly concerned about the disillusionment of young people with our world and with what adults have done to make it that way. We must support and help them to deal with their despair, their lack of meaning and their impotence. We can become their allies in transforming these feelings, which are not insurmountable and by which they do not deserve to be troubled. We must work to heal their wounds, as well as the problems of society which cause them. We can do still more. We can offer hope for the future, a promise of possible things to come, a rich expansive vision of how life can be and of what they may become.

Confucius said, 'What heaven has disposed and sealed is called the inborn nature. The realization of this nature is called the process. The clarification of this process is called education.' I am reminded of my recent experience of having a child and, I suspect, a universal experience of all parents — of seeing this tiny being as eternal, pure, undamaged promise. I saw this innocent new life as a symbol of hope for all human beings and their unquestionable potential for joy, for greatness, for beauty. This experience was in no way an idealistic fantasy, but actual truth, and I believe this symbol to be real. I invite you, the reader, to join me in a journey which seeks to add a vital ingredient to education.

I wrote this book from my heart and I ask you to read it from your heart. I deeply wish to motivate you to act, to do, to participate. This book is intended to be practical, inspiring and useful, rather than academic. The task we face as educators and parents requires more than a bunch of new techniques and exercises; who we are matters much more. Who we are means all aspects of ourselves, our gifts and qualities, our essential purpose in life, and our understanding of the profundity of human evolution.

What is this book really all about? What can it actually do for you and for the young person to whom it is dedicated? It is written in the spirit of wholeness; and it is intended for those who are interested and concerned, on a day-to-day basis, with the task of educating. This includes parents and more formal educators like teachers.* In it I hope to offer an enlarged understanding of human development and the uniqueness of each individual; while at the same time providing practical skills and techniques for working with the young person. The tools in this book have been widely practised and verified in schools and educational institutes in many countries. They are a product of the work of Dr Roberto Assagioli and of his students who continue to expand and elaborate his work.

This book is intended to help educators and young people in the following ways:

★ It demonstrates the importance of a well-rounded, balanced psychological development and suggests ways to stimulate the various functions such as coherent thought, imagination, feelings, will, creativity and the intuition.

★ It offers guidelines for both adults and young people, dealing with negative and problematic emotions at home and in the classroom.

★ It provides the ways and means for evoking and cultivating a spiritual awareness and vision of life.

It can help you to:

★ Improve interpersonal relationships with peers, family and teachers.

*Throughout this book when the term educator is used, I mean *both* teachers *and* parents.

★ Teach the child to take initiative and assert himself more in life.

★ Facilitate the creative confrontation of social issues.

★ Tackle the difficulties, the fears, and sense of inadequacy of you as an educator and provide a healthy perception of the young person.

★ Increase performance in school by showing ways in which the child can learn concentration and self-discipline.

Techniques and Exercises

This book contains many techniques and exercises to 'do' with young people, which to some will seem unusual or strange. Its theme is intended to be a complement to conventional education, *not* to suggest an alternative way; nor is its purpose to criticize that which is currently being offered. However, in spite of the breadth of current education, major human faculties, such as the imagination or the intuition, are still left underdeveloped. Some aspects of education have undoubtedly suffered from both a lack of attention and the non-availability of appropriate skills and tools. Others, such as learning to cope with destructive relationships or troubling social concerns, are not addressed at all.

Our young tend to evolve sporadically and without guidance, although it is being increasingly accepted that a natural evolutionary process exists. We can support this natural process of growth. Psychosynthetic education aims at developing and integrating the fundamental functions and qualities of the human being: physical, sensory, emotional, imaginative, ethical, social, volitional and transpersonal.

The exercises and techniques provided are neither mysterious nor complicated. With a basic understanding they are easy to implement; they are lively and playful with an emphasis upon creative expression, and young people enjoy the activity and involvement which they stimulate. A number of different modalities are used. We use drawing and art materials; we close our eyes and imagine things; we interact with one another, verbally and non-verbally; we write and think in a concentrated way; we make masks of psychological realities inside us; we dance and move around; we express and use our various sense functions. Upon completion of each exercise there are guidelines on how to use the experience in a constructive way, to integrate it into the participant's life.

Although the practice of the experiential work emphasizes play and creative expression, it is by no means lacking in depth and potency. The techniques are powerful and must be used consciously. Educators are advised to try out the exercises upon themselves, before using them with others. Only by doing so can we know what we are doing from the 'inside' and effectively introduce them to others. Guidelines and simple cautions are provided along the way.

The exercises are as much for the educator as for the child. They serve two purposes: one, to work on the content of the exercise; and two, to provide a context for people working together in a creative and nurturing way. We need to relate to young people on a deep and intimate level. The earlier we establish this context of knowing each other fully, the more we create our future relationships. If the ground is prepared for right human relationships early enough, in adolescence, they will not be estranged from us. What a child inherently longs for is the experience of unity and the intimacy of authentic relationships with the adult world.

Many adults today do not really know what to do with their children, and they busy themselves with outer events because of inadequacy and uncertainty. It is easier to buy a sophisticated toy, or go to the cinema, or watch television, than to be intimate with our child's inner world. However, the cost is great and our loss is the experience of truly knowing each other. Is it then surprising that we lose touch and our children increasingly feel like strangers to us, to themselves and to each other? What they really want is you: you in your human fullness, to be in contact with and close to. They want also to know your dreams and aspirations, your fears and doubts. They need to know that it is okay to be human, with the joys and struggles that this implies.

Humanistic and Transpersonal Psychology

In the late 1950s a radical shift occurred in the field of psychology, a shift which even today is not fully integrated into conventional psychology. It was the emergence of

Humanistic and Transpersonal psychology. Psychosynthesis,
which originated in 1911, gained further acceptance with this
larger development. The shift was a movement away from an
earlier tendency of psychology to limit itself to pathology, to
neurosis, to what was *wrong* with the human being, and
towards what the human being can become. The new
approach focused upon the evocation of potential and the
enhancement of what is beautiful and inherently positive in
man.

This idea of 'human potential' was first expressed by Dr
Abraham Maslow, an American psychology professor who
researched psychological health and studied self-actualized
people. He, Assagioli, and others, formulated a vision of what
a healthy, fully-functioning individual could be. They recognized that an integrated personality would have balanced
development of the psychological functions, an awareness of
human interconnectedness, and an awareness of the social
conditions most conducive to fostering potential. They
emphasized the power of the individual for self-regulation and
responsibility, while fully recognizing the interconnected
nature of mankind.

This Transpersonal essence, lying at the core of each of
us, is something which is beyond our everyday awareness,
beyond our egoistic impulses. It is what might be called the
true Self or the essential Self. It includes, but it is more than,
our personal day-to-day consciousness. From this Self we
discover meaning and the experience of having a purpose in
life, which often brings fulfilment. It knows who we are and
where we are going as well as what is worthwhile and of value
for us in life. As we work with this more spiritual level, we find
many important aspects of being human; such as acts of
altruism; the perception of beauty, and creative and artistic
impulses; the intuition; curiosity about the universe and our
place in it; and a sense of wonder and joy. Most young
children already demonstrate these qualities and do not need
to be taught them. On the contrary, our children could well be
our teachers and *our* task is to protect and to preserve these
inherent qualities. All too often we ignore, ridicule or
diminish them. Many of us may well remember the poignancy
of these experiences in our early years, but wonder where they
have gone.

Popular theories about children are many and varied; educators tend to change their attitudes with current trends, often leaving confusion in their wake. Are children devils or angels? Predestined or freewilled? A blank, unformed piece of clay or a predetermined character? Most of us have felt this ambivalence. Sometimes we experience the exquisite beauty of a child, which in precious moments is indeed angelic; and at other times we witness the exact opposite, for which the term devilish seems too mild. We can be struck by how in touch with life a child can be, how replete he is with elements that we have lost — like simplicity, spontaneity, creativity and awe. One has only to look into a child's eyes to be moved by his purity and presence.

On the other hand, some modern psychologists have seen the child as not more than a little animal, ruled or driven by impulses, instincts and fantasies of such a ferocious nature that they must later be repressed by social norms. This view perceives something in the child that is completely unruly and anarchistic, beyond good and evil, potentially destructive, requiring conditioning at best, controlling at worst. No one could deny the aggression and cruelty that is sometimes apparent in children's behaviour, especially towards other children.

This book addresses itself to *both* levels of humanness. We will see the beauty of the 'angel' and the violence of the 'devil'. Having a wider vision which includes *all* aspects of our experience of children, both so-called 'negative' and 'positive', is the only way we can honestly work. Effective education is only possible when we do.

The things a child will do in his life, and the experiences he will have, can be destructive or creative. This is both the depth of the responsibility, and the wonder of the opportunity, that educators have. If we imagine the myriad of actions and behaviours a child will eventually make in his life, the multitude of contacts he will have with other human beings, the vast array of forms of occupations available, and the variety of life experiences to be accrued, we may begin to grasp the importance that educators play in a young life. Education is a process which is continuous and limitless.

Chapter 1

WHAT IS PSYCHOSYNTHESIS?

The first impression that arises, when we look at contemporary psychology in its wider aspects, may well be one of contrast. On the one hand, sophisticated theories and rigorous research have contributed much to our knowledge of the human being; that knowledge, however, is often divorced from the art of effectively helping people to change. On the other hand, an increasing number of individuals, centres and schools are offering a wide variety of techniques to mobilize effectively psychological energies and evoke profound experiences. While these experiences are undoubtedly valuable, they are frequently left free-floating and unconnected. No satisfactory hypothesis is provided to take advantage of the wealth they offer.

As a global approach to human development, psychosynthesis aims to include the positive aspects of both positions. It acknowledges human experience in all its facets and, through the use of specific tools, seeks to expand it in quality and availability. It does not, however, abandon this inner process to the limbo of the unexplained, but clarifies its meaning by placing it within a flexible conceptual framework.

Another dichotomy occurs between the insights of mystics and creative individuals of all cultures and the findings of contemporary Western psychology. The latter has as a primary goal the creation of a normal, fully-functioning personality, but may ignore the higher realms of consciousness. Values, meaning, peak experiences, and the unquantifiable, ineffable essence of human life are often not addressed;

yet these are the very things to which spiritually-oriented people aspire. Nonetheless, higher states of consciousness are not by themselves a guarantee for effective psychological functioning and, when improperly handled, they can cause a wide variety of distortions and problems—a true pathology of the sublime.

Psychosynthesis attempts to acknowledge and harmonize both realms. On the psychological level it aims to build a personality which is free from emotional blocks, has command over all its functions and has a clear awareness of its own centre. On the transpersonal level, it enables the individual to explore those regions full of mystery and wonder beyond our ordinary awareness, which we call the superconscious: the wellspring of higher intuitions, inspirations, ethical imperatives, and states of illumination. This exploration culminates in the discovery of the Self, our true essence beyond all masks and conditionings.

The following is a diagram of Dr Assagioli's model of the totality of the human being.

1. Lower Unconscious
2. Middle Unconscious
3. Superconscious
4. Field of Consciousness
5. Conscious Self
6. Higher Self
7. Collective Unconscious

1. *The Lower Unconscious* corresponds to the unconscious in traditional psychology. This contains:
    a. The elementary psychological activities which direct the life of the body; the intelligent co-ordination of bodily functions.
    b. The fundamental drives and primitive urges.
    c. Many complexes charged with intense emotions.
    d. Various pathological manifestations incurred from various sources forming phobias, obsessions, compulsive urges and paranoid delusions.
2. *The Middle Unconscious* is formed of psychological elements similar to our waking consciousness, containing the memories, thoughts and feelings of which our everyday life is interwoven. This awareness is readily accessible to us merely

by tuning in or remembering. The middle unconscious contains recent or near present experiences or occurrences. It points not to what we have been or to what we could be, but to the rough evolutionary state we have actually reached. Dr Assagioli says that in this region our various experiences are assimilated with the ordinary mental and imaginative activities which are being elaborated and developed in a sort of psychological gestation, immediately before their birth into the light of consciousness.

3. *The Higher Unconscious or Superconscious* is the 'home' of our higher aspirations and intuitions, latent higher psychic functions, and spiritual energies. This includes artistic, philosophical or scientific, and ethical revelations and urges to humanitarian action. Dr Assagioli attributes the source of the higher feelings (such as altruistic love), of genius and of states of contemplation, illumination and ecstasy all to this realm. From the superconscious also come the impulses and energies that mould the evolution of the individual and of humanity collectively. Most of us have had, at some time, a moment of superconscious experience when we felt most fully who we essentially are, our 'true Self', our inner Godliness of a mystical, moral or aesthetic nature. Abraham Maslow would define such superconscious experiences as 'peak experiences' or experiences of transcendence. This neglected area of human experience is accorded much emphasis in the process of psychosynthesis.

4. *The Field of Consciousness* is that part of our personality of which we are directly aware. This includes the incessant flow of sensations, images, thoughts, feelings, desires and impulses, which we may immediately and consciously observe, analyse and judge.

5. *The Conscious Self or 'I'* is the centre of our consciousness, a point of 'I am I' or pure self-awareness. This 'I' is separate and distinct from the changing contents of our consciousness. This sense of 'I-amness' can be clearly experienced with careful introspection, or with the removal of the contents of our consciousness. If we remove such contents we are still left with a sense of continuity, a thread of sameness. This point of pure self-awareness, the 'I', is the essence of the being that remains unchanged from childhood through death.

6. *The Higher Self,* the Transpersonal Self or the Spiritual Self

is the point of pure essential Beingness which is above and unaffected by any conscious experiences. The Higher Self is not an experience; it is the 'One' who experiences, the Experiencer. The personal conscious self or 'I' is considered to be a reflection of the Higher Self and its projection in the field of the personality. It is said by Dr Assagioli to be the point of synthesis of the whole being, the more essential beingness of human existence.

7. *The Collective Unconscious* could be defined as the accumulated psychic environment that surrounds us. The boundary that separates us from it is permeable. 'It is analogous,' Dr Assagioli says, 'to the membrane delineating a cell, which permits a constant and active interchange with the whole body to which the cell belongs.' Such processes of 'psychological osmosis' are occurring all the time between human beings and the general psychic environment.

Concerning the use of psychosynthesis in education, Dr Assagioli himself says:

> It is axiomatic that the prevention of any disorder is better than its cure. If the techniques of psychosynthesis constitute effective therapy, as they do, how much better to prevent the need for later therapy by using psycho-synthetic techniques in early education? What, we wonder, are the implications of such a statement? Examining the type of education prevalent in the Western World from a viewpoint of: First producing a human being who functions harmoniously, radiantly and productively in relation to his own capacity. And second, establishing the conditions in which such an ideal could be realized.[1]

Dr Assagioli firmly believed this ideal to be recognizable and attainable, and he held to this throughout the lengthy development of psychosynthesis from 1911 to the present. He furthermore elucidated two major points which are essential and appropriate for a wider vision of educational goals:

1. The harmonious and well-balanced development of all aspects of the human being: physical, emotional, imaginative, intellectual, ethical, social and intuitive.
2. The integration of these characteristics into an organic synthesis, into a personality which is Self-conscious.

This vision includes developing *all* the functions of the child and helping him to discover and realize his true spiritual nature. Again to quote Dr Assagioli:

> Psychosynthesis is an inclusive and positive conception of man that considers him dynamically as a being in process, of personal growth within an evolving universe. It actively fosters the harmonious development of the emerging qualities within the human being, and their integration and synthesis around a higher unifying center. The scope of the psychosynthetic approach ranges from the personal, through the inter-personal to the universal and includes the Transpersonal dimension and superconscious processes.[2]

Chapter 2

THE TECHNIQUES OF
THE WORK

The experiential work of this book requires the educator and the participant to be willing to enter into an experience which may reach levels beyond the conscious mind. The purpose of using faculties, like the feelings, the imagination and the intuition, is to transform the learning process into an adventure, filled with the depth and richness these faculties provide. A child or adolescent learns most effectively when his whole being is actively engaged in his education.

Confluent education is the term used for the integration or *flowing* together of the cognitive and affective elements in individual and group learning. *Affective* refers to attitudes and values and to the feeling aspect of experience and learning. How an individual feels about wanting to learn, how he feels as he learns, and what he feels after he has learned, are all included in the affective domain. *Cognitive* refers to the activity of the mind in assimilating information. What an individual learns, and the intellectual process of learning, fall within this domain. The coherent integration of these areas is essential to meaningful and relevant education, to intelligent and mature behaviour, and to the individual taking a responsible and creative place in society.[1] Confluent educators are primarily interested in educating the child for life, evoking the wholeness which is his birthright, and fostering his *ability* to learn.

The experiential nature of this work takes the form of several different modalities through which to learn, the body and sensations, the world of feelings, the imagination and the intellect. Some modalities are more effective than others for different individuals; therefore the more modalities we include, the deeper and more productive is the learning. However, all these exercises are likely to enhance cognitive abilities as well as personal development.

Mental Imagery

Everyone uses visualization without even being aware of it; day-dreams, random fantasies and conscious imagining are a part of our everyday existence. If structured and consciously used, imagery and visualization can greatly facilitate the learning process. Their use does not require the educator to have extensive knowledge and training. However, they are potent techniques and should not be used indiscriminately. To quote Aldous Huxley on this subject:

> It is a matter of observable fact that all of us inhabit a world of fantasy as well as a world of first order experiences and a world of words and concepts. In most children and in some adults this world of fantasy is astonishingly vivid . . . For them the world presented to their consciousness by their storytelling, image making fantasy is as real, sometimes more real than, the given world of sense impressions and the projected world of words and explanatory concepts.[2]

Imagery may be simply defined as *seeing pictures in the mind*. Imagine trying to read without picturing what is written; doing a mathematical problem without seeing the symbols; or remembering something without vividly forming the important associations in the mind. Most learning occurs through imagining what is to be learned. If an individual cannot conceive of something in his mind it may be impossible for him to learn it in a lasting way.

This is not to say that short-term learning cannot take place through rote memorization, which is usually quickly forgotten. The ability to experience vivid imagery is strong and uninhibited in young children, but tends to wane as age increases. An obvious reason for this is that the imagination receives very little support or encouragement from the environment; moreover, it is often degraded and disapproved of and therefore inhibited. The typical school curriculum unfortunately does not include activities which encourage a student to use or develop it.

The validity of the imagination is nonetheless more widely accepted today. Fantasizing has been freed from the old misconception that it is useless or neurotic, and is being recognized as a valuable resource. Individuals who are willing to fantasize are found to understand themselves better, to live more imaginatively, to enjoy life more, to discriminate between fantasy and reality more readily, and to be less ruffled by unexpected thoughts or images.[3]

Imagery is not only the essential ingredient of all artistic creativity, but has also found its place in more scientific and mechanical processes. For example, the chemist Kekule had been working for a long time to find the structure of the benzene ring. One night he had an image of a snake eating its own tail. He was perplexed, but soon saw that the snake could well resemble the structure of the benzene ring and thus made his discovery.[4] Eli Whitney, who invented the cotton gin, made his discovery by observing a cat trying to pull a bird out of its cage. Every time the cat tried, the bird was held by the wires of the cage and the cat was left with only feathers. He translated the cat's experience to cotton plants and the possibility of pulling the cotton off the plant in a similar way—hence the cotton gin. A particularly famous example is Albert Einstein. At sixteen he had visualized himself riding through the universe on a beam of light, and the imagery started a process which years later led him to formulate the theory of relativity. These are a few of many examples of collaboration between logical creative thought and creative imagery.

Conscious or unconscious mental processes are as real as overt behaviour and can readily cause changes in that behaviour. Author and educator Richard de Mille believes that imagining can change behaviour as effectively as reasoning, willing or remembering.[5] Confluent educator Gloria Castillo also stresses the importance and function of imagination in the classroom. However, she makes the important point that emotions and fantasies can obstruct learning when they are uncontrolled. For example, a feeling or image that cannot be shared diverts the attention of the child's consciousness; or a feeling or an image that cannot be controlled is frightening to the child. Hence we can see the importance of providing structure and purpose to this imaginative process which is already occurring. She also says that the control of emotion and fantasy is essential for the attainment and discovery of knowledge *and* a prerequisite for the formation or invention of knowledge.[6] Obviously the wilful direction of the imagination is preferable to the destruction and repression of a precious human ability. Dr Assagioli wrote in his book *Psychosynthesis*:

> The imagination, in the precise sense of the function of evoking and creating images, is one of the most important and spontaneously active functions of the human psyche, both in its conscious and unconscious aspects or levels. Therefore, it is one of the functions which has to be controlled when excessive or dispersed; to be trained when weak; and to be utilised owing to its great potency.[7]

Mental imagery is the *language of the unconscious*. It allows us to communicate with our unconscious mind. By using mental imagery we are focusing our attention on and expanding our awareness of a particular area. Imagery gives us access to material that is not in our conscious mind but which resides in the vast reservoir of the unconscious. Canadian psychosynthesist Martha Crampton says:

> Just as the unconscious speaks to us in the language of images through dreams and fantasies, so we can address the hidden portions of our minds in this 'forgotten language', which is its native tongue.[8]

The exercises in this book use the imagination and work with the unconscious in two ways: by evoking or drawing out that which already exists in the unconscious, and by consciously reconditioning with images which are positive and life-affirming.

The Evocative Technique

Evoking is a process of consciously *calling up* an image or building an image of many elements representing a chosen area. It is a process that is carried out deliberately with a specific purpose, aimed at focusing awareness, enhancing development and integrating the various levels. The participant learns to *allow* images to come to mind in answer to certain questions. When using this type of imagery it is necessary to be relaxed for the formation of clear spontaneous images.

Allowing the unconscious to express itself freely through the imagination serves several purposes: it releases surplus energy, which if unreleased could have disturbing effects; it provides further awareness and understanding of that which is being focused upon; and it activates expression of latent creative potential. The value of this evocative technique does not depend entirely on interpretation. The participant may work through conflicts, for example between his body and feelings, or feelings and mind, on the imagined symbolic level, which can positively affect the actual level. This occurs whether or not he is able to understand intellectually or verbalize what has happened. His imaginings are better interpreted from his own experience than from the outside, and the increased awareness thereby gained often precipitates the process of change.

Reconditioning Techniques

Dr Assagioli suggests psychological laws of the psyche which state that, 'every image has in itself a motor drive or tendency' and 'images and mental pictures tend to produce the physical conditions and the external acts corresponding to them'.[9] If we are conditioned by our imaginings, which tend to manifest in reality, the structured and positive use of chosen images allows for the creation of corresponding psychological states. Symbols or images are *accumulators of psychic energy* carrying a *qualitative charge*. There exists a dynamic relationship between the symbol and the reality which it represents.

This relationship is based primarily on the analogous qualities between the symbol and reality, and when followed by analytical interpretation can bring rich insight. Selected images can be used in order to set into motion psychological processes as an effective means for transformation of the unconscious. For example, to visualize the *blossoming of a rose*, the unfoldment from bud to fully opened flower, can stimulate a similar profound reality in the human being. The same fundamental law of life governs the human mind as well as the processes of nature. In a similar way a child can *imagine* himself successfully performing a difficult or feared action and deeply increase his potential for doing so.

In addition, symbols further integrate the conscious and unconscious elements of the personality, and the rational mind with its irrational aspects. The imagination operates on several levels concurrently: sensation, feeling, thinking and intuiting. It provides a suitable way of training concentration and mental focus and, most importantly, requires the use of the will. In all exercises it is essential that we are not carried away by the imagination. We are using the imagination in a controlled and constructive way, in direct contrast to the everyday undisciplined wandering of day-dreaming. The process needs to be kept under our command and we should never lose the conscious feeling that we are in control. Participants need to spend adequate time in discussion and rational interpretation of the *meaning* of experiences they have had. The process of discussion provides the participant with freedom for expression, and the opportunity to share processes in symbolic form which might be too threatening to share in reality.[10]

The Technique of Free Drawing

Free drawing is a technique of psychosynthesis which is extremely effective for children and adolescents. The very act of drawing is a powerful expression of self and provides a way of expressing feelings. It entices the unconscious, which in certain respects has primitive and archaic traits, to express itself freely. Like imagery, it builds a bridge between the conscious self and unconscious elements and between the rational mind and its more irrational intuitive elements. It offers a means of expressing the contents of consciousness and of releasing repressed energy contained therein.

There are two ways of using this technique. In the first way the participant begins *playing* with paper and coloured crayons, allowing the hands to move freely and spontaneously. The correct attitude is simply to *let it happen*, just awaiting what will emerge. This method, if used to allow free expression of troublesome feelings, can release negative energy and liberate the child's consciousness for the task of learning.

The second way of using free drawing is to ask the participant to draw a particular image received during guided visualization. Such pictures need not be exactly reproduced. Students should be told to draw their *sense* or *feeling* of them, letting go of rationality as much as possible. It is the meaning that is hidden in colour, shape and feeling which is relevant to the work of free drawing and which brings learning and insight. When using free drawing it is essential to stress that it has nothing to do with art or art work. It is not an artistic endeavour at all. Often an objection made is, 'but I can't draw'. The answer is, so much the better, as any academic training in art would be likely to detract from the freeness of the drawing.

As with any experiential technique, it is fruitful to spend time afterwards in sharing and discussion among participants; and it is useful to invite them to share their drawings with one another, describing the pictures in their own way. What do the colours mean? Are they light or dark? What is the mood or tone of the drawing? Are any of the drawn shapes symbolic of real life situations or feelings? Is there movement or is it static? What is the hidden communication or message of the drawing? What does it tell you about yourself and your life? These types of questions bring into conscious awareness the insights that one is seeking.

The Technique of Meditation

Meditation can contribute to mental development, a clearer sense of identity, and spiritual unfoldment. Its use evokes that relaxed, purposeful and focused atmosphere which is an essential prerequisite for learning. Meditation is also a means for going beyond one's set patterns and mental habits by giving birth to new ideas and insights. Moreover, focusing the mind facilitates the strengthening of the will.

Meditation can be defined as a form of inner action. Far from being an escape from the world, as some believe, meditation can be a means of looking at it in a new and deeper way. By reuniting the inner and the outer universes it makes inner experience and outer perception and behaviour congruent, so that the child's energy is more available for learning.

Like all forms of practice, meditation requires discipline: one has to learn to use the mind in a conscious, deliberate way. It is also a matter of finding the appropriate mental tone: if we are mentally forceful or harsh, or if we over-identify with the intellect, our mind becomes rigid and crystallized. However, if we let our attention wander, we lose the capacity for clear and focused thinking. The meditative stage can be compared to holding a tiny bird in the hand. If held too tightly the bird will suffocate, if held too loosely it will escape.

Meditation can be used for many purposes in the classroom. Three types are particularly useful: reflection, symbolic imagery and silence.

Reflection

Reflective meditation requires directing the activity of the mind on the chosen topic. One learns to think deeply on a subject and examine all its ramifications, not just giving a superficial glance at one or two of its aspects.

The process by which the objective faculties of the mind are set aside allow it to become subjective, to probe in a deeper way than usual and to evoke intuitive understanding. By *deep thinking* on a subject one gains a clear, experiential idea about it and, through persistent and sustained attention, comes to know it *from the inside*.

There are two main areas for exploration through reflective meditation:

1. The various *transpersonal qualities* we desire to awaken or strengthen in ourselves, like courage, love, faith, serenity, joy, will, peace, cheerfulness, strength, openness, etc.

2. *Seed thoughts:* principles or ideas expressing a particular concept chosen to have value for the learning at hand. Some examples could be expressed by a statement, for example:

— Do we make history or does history make us?
— All that we are is the result of what we have thought.
— Do we manage computers or do they manage us?
— By what men fall by that they rise.
— Courage is mastery of fear, not absence of it.
— We are not troubled by things, but by the opinion we have of things.
— Experience is not what happens to us. It is what we do with what happens to us.

A useful variation of this technique is to choose a social issue or concern which holds the interest of a young person, and to reflect on the causes and possible resolutions of that particular issue, for example, racial discrimination, world hunger or nuclear disarmament.

Symbolic imagery

It is possible to use the imagination rather than the mind in meditative work. With closed eyes, the student is asked to visualize images with deep symbolic meaning and regenerative properties: the blossoming of a rose, the ascent of a mountain, a caterpillar that turns into a butterfly, dialogue with a wise and loving person, etc.

Symbols evoked with visualization work can be deepened and elaborated upon:

> Symbols properly recognized and understood possess great value; they are evocative and induce direct intuitive understanding. The fact that words indicating higher realities have their roots in sensuous experience serves to emphasize the essential analogical correspondences between the external and inner worlds.[11]

Meditation upon a positive symbol can greatly enhance the effect of that image on the unconscious, and may at times assist in resolving inner conflicts and in transforming negative tendencies into positive ones.

The use of the imagination is often pleasant and stimulating to the child, and allows this precious faculty to develop rather than atrophy—a sad destiny it often meets in traditional forms of education.

Silence

Silence involves the stilling of thought, openness and availability to insight, and a wordless *waiting* for creative inspiration to break through into consciousness.

Some elementary form of silence was introduced in some schools many years ago. Maria Montessori experimented with the use of silence in the early part of this century, and now in most Montessori schools silence is used regularly. The success of this method is illustrated in a statement of a Montessori teacher:

> We have yet to accept and act upon the axiom that the cultivation of a habit of silence is an integral part of all true education; and that children, so far from looking upon a demand for silence as an unnatural and intolerable imposition, have an inborn aptitude for quietness. To

realise the truth of this, one need only witness the silent time in a Montessori school. The blinds are drawn, the signal is given, and each little head is bowed as a happy stillness, free from any morbid taint, descends upon the children. It is a real silence, not lazy half-dozing. Something akin to true meditation takes place . . . there is a hint of depth in the merry eyes, a suggestion of more than physical health and peace in their whole body.[12]

A psychosynthetic-trained teacher in a state school in London uses 'a moment of going to our special quiet place' as a regular part of her daily routine with young children in primary classes, and finds that the children respond positively.

Receptive silence can be facilitated by combining it with guided visualization: the educator guides the student through the visualization to enable him to become more focused in his silence. The meditator holds the idea or subject under consideration in his mind with closed eyes, and imagines the sun shining down on it; or he holds an image of the subject of meditation to the light and allows it to be transformed.

Following receptive meditation it is beneficial for the meditator to take notes of its results and conclusions. Writing also serves as a means of articulating the experience and making its content more real and available later. It also stimulates the intuition, and it is a way of grounding: insights gained through receptive meditation tend to fade quickly from the conscious mind if they are not recorded.

There are several meditations in the transpersonal exercise section with detailed instructions for their use.

Some Guidelines For Experiential Work

To act as a *guide* in the exercises in this book, the educator needs to know only a few basic guidelines and principles in order to facilitate the work of children and adolescents. The participants may not be accustomed to working in a mode that uses more than the rational mind, and it may take a little time and practice for them to become familiar with this way of working. Younger children tend to adopt these exercises naturally as they are a focused extension of play. Adolescents consistently respond well to the more innovative and active participation required by the exercises, and any initial awkwardness is usually followed by enthusiasm.

Motivate the participant

A willingness to participate and become involved is a necessity. We cannot expect children and adolescents to follow our instructions blindly, therefore it is wise to explain the purpose of whatever experiential work being done. Educators, aided by having done the exercise themselves previously, have found it helpful to evoke motivation to participate by creating an atmosphere of excitement, which participants will find contagious.

Physical relation

All of the suggested exercises are both effective and enjoyable if a brief body relaxation precedes them. This may be enough just to stand up and stretch, or shake the body to wake it up; a few minutes of relaxed concentrated breathing may be suggested, or a mentally-induced moment of silence. In all the exercises the body should be in a comfortable posture.

Voice and language

It is advisable to guide the experiences in a calm, soothing tone of voice. The way to discover one's best voice is to say the exercise to yourself first, relax and cultivate the tone of voice that feels most suitable. A way of speaking that sounds harmonious to you will probably be appropriate for the participants. The words and images may be varied according to the age and maturity of the participants. The exercises themselves may also be changed in any way that seems appropriate.

Individual variations

It may seem surprising that the ability to visualize is not uniform among children, adolescents or adults. Some will report having mental imagery that is sharp and clear, in vivid colours and enduring; while others are limited to grey tones with less clarity. Rarely will a child say he cannot visualize at all. When guiding participants through the exercises, individual differences in the ability to visualize may be noted, but they do not constitute an obstacle. Each of us imagines in our own unique way and can be encouraged to do so accordingly. Some do not see pictorial images but rather *sense* or *feel* the experience. Some children may need reassurance that their way is acceptable, for there is no *right* way to visualize.

Eyes
Certain people obtain the best results by visualizing with their eyes closed; others with eyes open. The more extroverted person may find visualizing with the eyes closed most successful, as open eyes tend to bring in distractions to concentration, while closing the eyes encourages them to introvert and direct attention to the inner world. On the contrary, an extremely introverted person will have more difficulty with closed eyes, as their interest is already directed inwards, with other images or psychological processes crowding their attention. We should allow the participant to determine which way works best for him.

No rules of reality
The world of the imagination does not follow the rules of reality. This point needs to be made explicit for participants in guided visualization. Children are usually delighted to learn this and be given permission to let themselves go. Images may be given the power of speech and movement, impossible things may happen, illogical and irrational stories or scenes may emerge, inanimate objects may come alive—absolutely anything is possible in the world of the imagination. For example, we can talk to images and communicate with our body in a way that in reality is not possible—a dragonfly can take a bath, a flower can speak, a stone can fly or a house destroy and rebuild itself. With guided imagery, the creative myth-making, story-telling function of the unconscious is at work.

Attitude of the guide
The *attitude* of the guide can be encouraging and supportive to the participant. Educators can help the individual to master both the real and the imaginary world by allowing him full expression of his experience outside the structured exercise. In interpersonal communication, full expression depends partly on a demonstration of full appreciation by the listener. This appreciation should be general and explicit, through active listening and positive acceptance of the participant's experience.[13]

We may encounter a participant feeling embarrassed or behaving in a *silly* manner when first doing experiential work. This occurs most among younger children, but is easily dealt with by acknowledging the embarrassment and communicating our understanding of it. When under way the techniques create their own discipline, and the guide does not have to worry. A study was done in which meditation was taught to children in a New York public school. The population of the school happened to be rather aggressive. Nevertheless the techniques were successful and once the initial silliness subsided, the children responded very well.[14]

Grounding the Experiences

The time spent following an exercise is as important as the exercise itself, otherwise the experiential work may remain at the level of unarticulated awareness. To gain the deepest effects, the *content* and results of the exercises require elaboration and interpretation. The analytical rational mind is a useful tool for understanding the insights and for applying them to daily life. A bridge can be built between what happened in the exercise and what it means in terms of our knowledge of ourselves and our life in the world. Martha Crampton, proponent of guided imagery work in schools, says:

> An intellectual formulation, provided it is not an intellectualization and does not precede or substitute for emotional and intuitive insight, seems to consolidate and make more complete the process of understanding. It may be possible to facilitate the transfer of learning from one situation to another and make behaviour patterns more accessible to conscious direction.[15]

Each child should be encouraged to share and discuss his experience. If the educator opens up and shares his own experience, participants will tend to do likewise. For example, if the educator says, 'With that exercise I got an image of a barrel full of water for my body, and this tells me that my body needs to be appreciated more', the participant will experience that he too can share his image and what it means to him.

A participant should never be forced to share something if he really does not want to. The educator must avoid interpretations, but can check out guesses and hunches with the individual. If he's not willing or interested in responding, that's fine. Unclear or uneasy feelings or inner conflicts should be addressed, and as much as possible resolved. Often, sharing and *talking things through* tends to accomplish this. The participant needs to have his experience recognized, accepted and received as *real*, with compassionate understanding. Simple suggestions may be made and often answers are contained within the experience itself.

It is useful to relate guided imagery experiences to the *here and now* and to everyday reality, in reaching for explicit awareness. The participant should be asked in what way the emotional quality of his experience is similar to experiences in his daily life, whether his experience reminds him of anything familiar, any person in his life or any life situation that can bring insightful connections. Other useful questions to ask following an exercise might be:

What was that experience like for you?

Does it fit with you and your life?

Who would like to share what happened?

Were there any surprises?

Did you learn or discover anything about yourself?

How do you feel about what happened?

How do you feel now?

What do you think that means?

Did you like what happened?

How would you have liked it to be different? How can that happen?

Have you experienced anything like it before?

What did it remind you of?

What does your experience mean in terms of your everyday life?

How can you use what happened to understand yourself better?

In order for each child to have the opportunity to express himself and share the results of his experience, it may be necessary to form smaller groups(two to six people). Sharing in these smaller groups gives the opportunity to develop communication skills with peers and leads to empathy and positive acceptance. Often a child or adolescent is surprised to discover that others have similar experiences and difficulties in their lives. This realization can be liberating, bringing home the reality that he is not alone with his struggles and problems, which in turn encourages him to open up and share more of his inner world.

Warmth and positivity is the best atmosphere for this kind of communication. The educator can contribute to this atmosphere by authentically communicating his own inner realities. Both positive and negative experiences should be shared, but emphasis can be put on the positive, growthful aspects. This can be achieved by emphasizing the positive alternative, or by searching for a positive alternative, to negative aspects that emerged. I often find that another child is the best resource for helping to resolve difficulties. Children and young people naturally tend to help each other through difficult experiences, intuitively and skilfully.

Occasionally, and a vast amount of classroom experience has shown it to be only occasionally, a child may have an extremely negative experience, which reveals deeper psychological problems. This must be noted and appropriate action taken, outside the classroom or at home, possibly through a school counsellor or parental involvement. In some instances, only the true understanding of an adult is needed; while other problems may require further intervention. Rather than the child continuing to cope alone, it is much better that the problem has been brought into the open where proper help and support can be provided.

Chapter 3

GROWING UP WHOLE

Much of the growth and development of a child is mysterious and complex and is neither obvious nor readily available to interpretation. However, some knowledge of the various psychological levels through which a child may pass, and an ability to assess where a child is in relation to them at any time, will enhance our effectiveness as educators. We can do much to enrich and nurture a child's development; but we may also unwittingly thwart or diminish it. The process in every child is different and unique, but we require only a fundamental understanding of his personality structure to add the positive and encouraging ingredients to his education. We do not need to be psychologists. We do need to open our hearts and minds.

In this chapter I will define the child's personality structure by subdividing it into the body, the feelings and the mind. This distinction is not absolute. It is simply a way of providing a perspective when confronted with the immensity of a child's learning, growth and development. They might be described as personality aspects, functions or levels of experience. These aspects are not really separate, although it is useful for us to talk about them as if they were, as each has different functions and all three need to be addressed in the educational process if it is to be complete.

As life unfolds, emphasis shifts, at different times, onto one or another of these aspects. Although it is difficult to say when this emphasis occurs, we can be sensitive to it in order to relate appropriately to a child at any stage. This is important so that he will experience being seen, heard and understood. We have all known the pain of not being 'met', of being misunderstood at a critical moment, of longing to have our inner reality affirmed. For example, when the body is in a period of accelerated growth, a child's consciousness will be more focused there. When a child is learning how to read he will be much more focused in his mind. The turmoil of an adolescent's emotional life may, for a time, seem to exclude the mind. The emphasis changes frequently and may even change within the course of a day. A child's development is not complete until the development of each aspect (body, feelings, mind) is also complete. A child should learn to play each one of these 'instruments' easily and skilfully and find himself 'at home' in each, rather than developing one dimension at the expense of others. The normal educational process tends to focus exclusively on mental development.

Our body, with its impulses, drives and instincts, is the most solid, tangible and visible part of ourselves. As with all animals it must develop and mature in order for us to survive. We may imagine that our body will take care of its own development and in part this is true; yet a child may have a multitude of feelings and attitudes towards his body that will affect its development. At the beginning of our life our attitude towards the physical dimension is natural and positive. However, whether this naturalness remains will depend upon the experiences we have in early years. Less healthy attitudes and perceptions such as fear and rejection may be learned. Some children unconsciously feel that there is something *wrong* with the physical dimension of life; they become clumsy with it, or imagine it to be base and unclean.

Our feeling world is much more subjective, intangible, and of all three aspects it is the one that lacks most definition. It is the aspect of ourselves that is the most changeable and it is where trouble strikes most often. Because they are invisible and intangible, we don't take care of our feelings with the same urgency that we do if our body is ill. Just as there is physical 'energy', so there is emotional 'energy'. This energy can be used, channelled and transformed to add great depth to learning if we, as educators, are skilful enough.

The functions of the feelings are to provide power and colour to whatever we do, to vitalize ideas, to reflect intuitions, to facilitate communication, and to provide us with depth in human experience.

We have already noted that conventional education focuses extensively upon the mind and particularly on cognitive learning, about which much is known. I will focus on those aspects of mental functioning not normally addressed. The world of thought is made up of mental construct, opinions, beliefs and attitudes, which I will be addressing. It is generally not acknowledged that our mind is sometimes governed by our feeling state rather than having an independence of its own. So, for example, when the mind is coloured by feelings, it ceases to be clear and objective and may show prejudices. However, the opposite is also true. The mind can overpower feelings, ignore and violate them.

The following functions of the mind are particularly important for educators: to understand and correlate ideas, to order and organize in concrete and practical terms, to grasp meaning and to define, to formulate plans, to envision and to create new realities.

The Body

Naturally our body is the first phase of our development. An infant's awareness is primarily concerned with the body— hunger, bodily functioning, comfort, etc. This early development of the organism is appropriate, for our body is the first thing that must mature in order for us to survive. The farther back in time we reflect, the more physical are our memories. If we observe young children we see that a major thrust in their life is physical, with a fascination for all the physical aspects of reality.

The main function of the body is to locate us in the world and give us mobility. It is well equipped with the tools and functions for its own sustenance, survival and protection. By and large these systems are efficient, reliable, and do not require much development beyond that provided by the environment, though our bodies can be trained to perform prodigious feats. However, a fully functioning body is vital as a means of expression, of comunication with others, and for the enjoyment of physical sensation and experiences. These abilities or functions are also less developed than they might be and their potential is seldom realized.

A major learning process is the development of physical self-control. Through physical contact our awareness of other people and objects increases, aided by the mastering of motor capacities. We can watch a small child constantly exploring the physical world, ceaselessly manipulating shapes and forms.

Throughout much of early childhood we continue to use our body to find out about the world, although feelings and mind are developing peripherally. Our body and our senses serve the mind; and the mind expresses itself through physical action. Without the five senses, our minds would be woefully inadequate. To acknowledge the body as a foundation for the mind emphasizes the importance of encouraging the full unfoldment of this function.

The process of the development of the body is one of refinement from gross to subtle. The first movements or efforts at physical expression are gross and undifferentiated, but as time passes a child learns increasing subtlety and dexterity in dealing with the physical universe. As differentiation takes place the body becomes more co-ordinated and expressive. By late childhood, seven to nine years of age, if his development is relatively normal, a child can move and use his body nearly as well as an adult.

The benefits of a healthy body
What are the benefits of having a healthy, fully functioning body? For a moment, let us envisage what the ideal model of this health would be like. We would see:

— A connectedness with the world of nature and the physical universe;
— Physical health, a love and appreciation for the body and good maintenance;
— Good capacity for expression through the body, through voice, gesture and facial movements;
— The development of physical skills and the capacity to do things well with the hands;
— A greater capacity for enjoyment and enhanced sensory awareness, thus eliminating boredom;
— Good respect and care for objects;
— A positive self-image with the confidence that accompanies it;

— A capacity to liberate energy that is encapsulated in the body through past emotional traumas and experiences, so that psychological problems are not retained in the body;
— The ability to experience higher states of consciousness through the body and to feel the body as the home of the Self.

To quote the seventeenth-century philosopher Spinoza, 'Teach your body how to do many things and you'll become capable of the love of God.'

The benefits of encouraging the complete growth and expression of the body are obvious. By reinforcing and affirming this development we can minimize future imbalances and disharmonies. Basic issues will arise which are sometimes defined as instincts, for example, the quest for nourishment and for successful establishment of contact with the environment. If these instincts are frustrated or degenerated on the physical level, deep emotional problems can result; if they are inhibited on the psychological level by environmental, parental or educational constraints problems arise which plague the person later in life.

For example, if for some reason there is insecurity in connection with nourishment—food being withheld as punishment or given as a reward—a more generalized behaviour of hoarding or over-eating may develop. A fear of not being adequately nourished may later lead to an emotional and mental component within this pattern. Another example we often encounter is the child's attitude towards his body. If he implicitly receives a message that his body is something not to be touched or explored, and that it is basically naughty to be too interested in it, he may grow to feel ashamed of his body and become self-destructive. I once worked with an adolescent who had, throughout childhood, been told that she was clumsy and awkward physically, and her self-image had been severely damaged in consequence. She had withdrawn from participation in any activity that required using her hands.

'I was never any good at sports' is the explanation offered by many adults, who were to their detriment prematurely labelled as unathletic by an impatient educator. If a child's need for love and attention is not directly met by the environment, he may accidentally discover that when ill he receives the much-needed attention and, over a period of time, may unconsciously become prone to illness. Any of these already-distorted behaviours can become generalized patterns, which also affect other areas of consciousness. Deep complexes may be formed which only show up later in life.

From this it should be clear that through our behaviour and attitude towards a child's physical life we can either build healthy physical functioning or plant the seeds for future disruptions.

The Feeling Life

While the formative value of a child's feelings is generally greater than we tend to realize, they are further awakened and emotional development is accelerated with the onset of puberty and adolescence. New energies, new feelings, new thoughts, ideas and opinions are presenting themselves. The personality is asserting and forming itself. Contacts with the environment and people which characterized the preceding time, assume a different character; they become more varied and differentiated; they acquire new emotional qualities, and sometimes a spiritual note is discernible. This phase can be likened to that of a chrysalis in process of transforming itself into a butterfly. The process unfolds throughout adolescence and into young adulthood.

The development of the feeling life

Whereas the development of the body is largely extroverted, feeling development is more introverted. This enrichment of inner life deepens the experience of play and contact with other human beings. Whereas younger children play side by side and then learn to play *with* each other, play now begins to take place on more levels. For example, a child may select a role in a game that enables him to vent a dominant feeling. Also in play the dynamic of the interpersonal relationship becomes more important than the activity itself. Rich nuances emerge and by adolescence many shades of subtle meaning are manifesting. This shift in focus is also reflected in language, which takes a quantum leap parallel to feeling development.

The developmental issues at this time are primarily those of relatedness, acceptance, inclusion and group membership. Concern emerges about how one is perceived by others and how one perceives others. Self-assertion and a searching for some form of identity and independence become apparent. These issues are of major significance and the adolescent may not be aware of it himself. (They are the subject of deeper consideration in a subsequent section of this book, see Chapter 6 'Adolescent Identity Struggles'.) By way of illustrating this, recall your teenage years when your feelings were so intense. Think of how powerful your emotions were at that time—the agony of having a pimple—or your mouth not being the right shape—or the fact that Joe didn't talk to you that day—or not having the right dress on—or not getting invited to that party . . . . The string of minor events producing major emotional reactions is endless. Every adolescent passes through the fire of emotional development, though each will experience it in his own unique way.

Feelings and learning
I am not implying that educators should play therapist with the emotions of young people. I am suggesting, however, that they should have some understanding of emotions and feelings, be able to make the distinction between them, and to realize how feelings can aid cognitive learning. Feelings are multi-dimensional, containing elements of imagination, of instinct, of intuition and of impulse, and, of course, of physical and sensational experience. An emotion is a qualitative interpretation that we attribute to the combination of experiences. For example, if I am sad about my grandmother's death, I may have a lump in my throat and tears in my eyes, feel a sense of loss, resent her for leaving me, have fantasies about life in the past with my grandmother or fears about life without her in the future, and have an impulse to run to her home town. These are all feelings; the emotion is sadness.

Feelings obviously can deepen and elaborate learning. The child who learns with all of his resources will find education enjoyable, rich and alive and, most importantly, more long lasting. The educator who can engage the young person's feelings will gain their reward in terms both of exam results and of the quality of their own relationship with their students.

In some ways feelings are the common denominator between us in our day-to-day living, in our relationships to each other and in learning together. The mind, of course, is recognized as the major instrument of education, but beneath it is the world of feeling which is all too often ignored. Unconsciously we are all preoccupied with feeling states: wanting to feel happy, good; feeling bad and wanting to change that; seeking emotional gratification; reaching out for our needs to be met; searching for approval and self-esteem. To acknowledge the importance of feelings is to honour an implicit knowing that each of us has the right to see and be seen, to hear and be heard, to touch and be touched, to understand and be understood.

The richness, vividness, colour and depth of life is provided by our feelings. It is the 'juice of life'. The vast number of feeling states that can be experienced are a rich resource and yet at the same time they can interrupt the learning process and block us. Psychosynthesist Piero Ferrucci describes it in this way:

> If we take a closer look at the situation, we clearly see that feelings are a necessary ingredient in everyone's life: they are an inexhaustible source of enjoyment, they facilitate communication, they add power and colour to whatever we do, they vitalise ideas and reflect intuitions. And yet just following our feelings may subject us to invasion by other individual's emotions; distort our perception of the world; cause us to fall into prejudice, confusion and hysteria; let us be tortured by excessive sensitivity; and stimulate regression to our ancestral past. The point, clearly, is that we cannot trust our feelings indiscriminately, as if they were oracles: to do so might lead us astray. On the other hand, we cannot disparage them because that would repress a precious dimension of our being.[1]

Ferrucci recommends caution because the psychological elements that we consciously suppress or unconsciously repress do not 'sit quietly in the basement'. They continue to try to enter our awareness and behaviour either covertly or directly; and they deaden our life energy, stopping us from being fully present with whatever activity we are engaged in. But the most exuberant, unwanted emotions can be transmuted towards more desirable and effective expressions. An individual who has healthy and well-developed feelings is more likely to be self-aware or conscious.

A task of education is to help the young person become more aware of himself, to enable him to feel strong within himself, and see the world as it really is. He needs to know he has choices about how he lives and about how he reacts, and that he can be responsible for making these choices. The relationship between educator and child is absolutely crucial during this time. Educators themselves need to be aware of the quality and intensity of their *own* feelings in order to respond appropriately to the feelings of others.

Young children do not place blame for their limitations or problems upon their parents or the outside world. We could say that they live in a state of emotional participation with life. They imagine *themselves* to be bad, that *they* have done something wrong, that *they* are not clever enough, articulate enough, pretty enough or whatever. Children who feel 'bad' find ways to protect themselves. Some withdraw into their inner world in order to avoid getting hurt; some conform and behave exactly as expected and are over-pleasing and good; some become fearful of everybody and everything; and some work and learn 'as if' nothing were the matter, shutting out what is painful. Some children will strike out with extremely negative aggressive or hostile behaviour because it is the most effective means they know of getting the attention they crave. In an attempt to take care of his needs, each child will have developed a unique way of coping. Children do what, in their childlike consciousness, seems necessary in order to get through and survive. In the face of any interruption in their natural functioning they will unconsciously choose the particular behaviour that seems to serve them best.

With any individual child we can assess his way of coping and adjust our behaviour towards that child accordingly. If we can perceive the need behind his behaviour, we have the opportunity to meet that need in healthy ways, while encouraging and teaching the child to reach out appropriately for what he needs. We can help him to recognize that he has options available of which he was previously unaware. One of the hardest things for older children to learn is to be straightforward with their feelings. They need to relearn how to ask directly for what they want, and to say what they like and dislike. They probably did this as little children, but sadly in the process of enculturation they all too often learn to repress rather than express their feelings.

Obviously the educator's attitude and behaviour, both as a role model and as a facilitator, is vitally important. His emotional fluidity, state of psychological health and relationship with the feeling function, determine what is both implicitly and explicitly communicated in the classroom. The collective reality of the classroom means that children pick up what is acceptable or not acceptable to their educator, and this influences their inner life as well as their outer behaviour. In the long term this overall dynamic affects a child's future relationship with his emotional life and his sense of self-worth.

Working with feelings
The next question is how? How can we as educators maintain the educational process while respecting the feeling life of the young person? Psychological health, like education, is a lifetime process of learning, and there are no recipes or simple directions to follow. We can, however, develop a fundamentally healthy attitude towards the feelings of children by our acceptance of them and by refraining from unnecessary judgement or interpretation of them.

There are some basic guidelines which educators have found useful for integrating the affective domain into the classroom, *and* at home. The process is:

1. To become aware of what it is.
It is not always immediately obvious to the child what feelings he is experiencing or how to define them. More often he is unconscious of the content of his experience, and awareness may need to be encouraged. There will be visible cues or signs that demonstrate the emotion and sometimes a simple question like, 'What do you feel right now?' can bring the necessary awareness. Giving direct feedback through observation also evokes awareness. For example, 'I see you're looking sad', or 'I notice that you're clenching your fists', or 'It seems you're holding your breath', or 'I see you frowning', and 'I bet you're angry'. This type of simple direct observation and feedback is potent.

Once a feeling is identified, further elaboration and description can be called upon by asking more questions such as, 'Where in the body do you experience it? What size is it and what is its intensity on a scale of one to five? What colour is it?' The purpose of these questions is to increase the child's awareness of his feelings, not for the educator to analyse them. Awareness leads to a greater understanding and experience of a feeling, its meaning and its impact. Its evoked expression leads to the dissipation of the charge it carries. Every emotion has a corresponding body experience and corresponding thought.

2. To accept and to include what is.
If we examine the usefulness of accepting our feeling life, we are immediately confronted with a paradox. Feelings should be taken seriously, as we may readily experience the painful consequence of not doing so, with its accompanying loss of aliveness; and, interpersonally, if we do not respect the feelings of another he will not feel accepted and understood. On the other hand, feelings should not be taken too seriously. The credibility of feelings could be questioned, as they are indeed constantly changing and are often the result of our distorted perceptions and emotional instabilities. The transitoriness of a feeling is evident if we were to review, in retrospect, any one day of our life to see the multitude and diversity of our emotions. Feelings are not oracles of truth and we need to cultivate a perspective of right proportions. This is especially relevant for adolescents, where the fire of feeling life can be quite overwhelming. Encouraging right proportions, clear perception and a healthy balance between feeling and thinking functions, is a lesson to be learned for each of us. In younger children, it is our attitude and behaviour towards their own feelings that will facilitate this learning.

Feelings are not static; they are constantly changing. To allow a feeling to be, is to allow it to change. Given that denial or repression is not effective, we must somehow communicate to the child that whatever he is feeling is acceptable. Acceptance is not passive resignation but simply a recognition of a momentary reality. Psychologically to allow a feeling to exist enables the process to move on, or the experience to pass. Much energy can be wasted if, for example, a child is trying hard to push away or deny the feelings he does have. If the educator can help the child to recognize and then accept his experience as a natural occurrence, the process unfolds and there is no loss of potential. This demands a non-judgemental attitude from the educator, a state to which he may not be accustomed. He must refrain from rationalizing or interpreting the experience. He simply must *let it be*.

All too often the educator will not enquire into what is wrong or troubling a child for fear of opening up a whole can of worms. If a child is disruptive he is often punished, kept in, shouted at; or at least is given a good *talking to*. The educator may feel angry at the child for disrupting the class, and resent his troublesomeness. Often the educator uses his authority to enforce conformity or *good* behaviour and to convince the child to deny the importance of his experience, thereby excluding his reality and rendering him impotent. The implicit message is, 'your feelings do not matter'.

I will illustrate this point with an example. A class was busy with a group project that the children were especially enthusiastic about. The teacher noticed that one child was somehow pushed out of the activity and was standing to the side looking quite lost and forlorn. The teacher stopped the activity briefly, asking the children what they felt was going on here. She asked the child who had been pushed out how he felt about being outside the activities. He replied quite easily and consciously that he felt angry and hurt—for having been pushed out. The child who had pushed him out was totally unaware that he had done so—in the excitement of the moment it had happened inadvertently and the pushing child was quite surprised to discover this. He immediately made room for the child outside the circle to return and the situation was resolved easily. Nothing else needed to be done. The key factor in the resolution of this situation was for the child that had been pushed out to include and express directly *then and there* what he was feeling.

This is a very different thing from the teacher resolving the situation, either through her authority or through convincing the child to come back to the activity. A repressive way of dealing with this same situation would have been to push aside the child's hurt and anger by smoothing over it, or not taking it seriously, or telling the child not to be so silly—all reactions which would have *excluded* the child's reality.

The following is another example, told in the words of one of our teachers:

> Susan's rabbit had died from the cold and she had found it just before school. She came into the class crying and very upset. I held her and said I could see she was feeling very sad. She told me about the rabbit. I stayed with her for a while and then when the rest of the class had come in I told them about Susan's rabbit . . . how it had died last night and how as they could see, Susan was feeling very sad and upset. I asked her what she wanted to do and she said to sit down quietly. She was still crying. I said to the class that we all could help Susan today. She might feel upset during the day when she remembered her rabbit and might feel like crying, and that would be okay. . . . (It is necessary to remind children that it is alright to cry because with a lot of teachers it isn't.) Susan remained quiet during the day but seemed to naturally move through her sadness. No further work was necessary.

Here again are some typical repressive attitudes that an educator might have had:

1. 'Oh dear, Susan, how sad. Well sit down now and get on with your work.'
2. 'Never mind, you'll soon forget him.'
3. 'Never mind, I expect your parents will get you another one.'
4. If the crying had continued for a few minutes: 'Don't make a fuss. You're not an infant. Try and act grown up.'

3. After acceptance: What to do?

It is vital to avoid the repression or unnecessary limitation of feeling awareness and expression. However, it is equally important not to release feelings in inappropriate ways, which can have destructive consequences. We have all had experiences of both the constructive and destructive side of emotional expression, which has left us confused and uncertain about what is appropriate, when, and how. There is no simple recipe for dealing with feelings once we have recognized and accepted them.

It is necessary to allow a child to become *conscious* of his feelings, to *know* them. This is an essential first step in helping children to experience being strong and whole rather than running away, avoiding or discharging feelings in indirect ways which can cause both harm to themselves and others. Next a child must learn the skill of evaluating the situation and determining a choice regarding how to respond and behave. A child does need to learn to be able to express what he is feeling when that is appropriate *or* at other times to be able to contain his feelings. Ultimately he needs an inner freedom from which to choose appropriate behaviour. Choice is the key factor. The possibility to choose expression or containment at any given moment brings inner freedom. A more elaborate explanation of this all-important 'choice' factor is included in the chapter on the will.

Expression of Feelings

Life in the classroom provides an excellent laboratory for the acquisition of the skill of responsible behaviour. Depending upon the situation, when feelings arise, a child *can be encouraged* to communicate what he is feeling to the person involved. The best way of dealing with a momentary disturbance in the classroom is the direct way, by asking those concerned to express their feelings, explain their point of view, encouraging them to listen to others, and helping them to consider how else they might have responded or behaved.

Behind every disturbance there is likely to be an unfulfilled need. The overt behaviour of a child is merely his way of seeking fulfilment of that need, but the need often goes unnoticed, is rarely responded to, and seldom fulfilled. If the child can become conscious of what he truly needs at any moment he can make choices to meet that need, which are perhaps more constructive and not dependent upon the previous behaviour. There are usually many alternative ways to meet the deeper need, which provide the kind of flexibility necessary for constructively dealing with feeling problems.

An area where children are usually able to recognize a need is in their interpersonal relationships. For example, a common occurrence is for a child to be either very sulky, moody, sad, crying—or to be disruptive, messing around, angry and not working. When we evoke the child's needs through our questioning, we are likely to hear replies like: 'I want to be friends with . . . or . . . doesn't like me . . . or won't play with me . . . or I haven't any friends'; in this way a child's needs for friendship and inclusion become clear.

Sometimes our questioning may bring answers which demonstrate a need for security or support that cannot be entirely met in the classroom. For example: 'My mum and dad were arguing last night' or, 'My mum/dad left home' or, 'My mum/dad said they're leaving'. Here, too, giving the child involved a chance to talk about how they feel, and share it with either educator or the class, gives him space and acknowledges the child's valid need, which can be partially met through expressing it in a loving understanding environment. How can a child who is worrying about whether or not his parent will be home that evening be able to work?

On this point I would like to relate a specific example taken from the classroom of a psychosynthesis teacher who works with fourteen- to sixteen-year-olds. There was a particular boy, let's call him Joe, whose behaviour was consistently disruptive and difficult. Joe was either hyperactive in his behaviour or he was totally depressed and withdrawn, refusing to join in classroom activities. Either way, his behaviour or non-behaviour stopped the work from continuing. Joe obviously needed to have attention focused on him at all times and would succeed in getting it, usually by playing the class *fool* or clown, or through aggressive actions.

The teacher decided, one day, to confront this problem head on by giving Joe attention—before he had reverted to his outrageous behaviour. She asked the class to sit in a circle and invited Joe to become the centre of attention directly, and Joe with both surprise and delight agreed. She began by acknowledging to Joe that it appeared that he really needed the class's attention but the problem with his behaviour was that, although his disruptive behaviour got him attention, it also prevented the class from doing anything else. She gave him direct and clear feedback about his holding the whole class back. How did he feel about it?

Joe smiled and began to talk about himself in a general way, about his hopes and dreams and fears. . . . After a few minutes the teacher asked class members if they would give Joe some feedback on how they felt about him. Some of the feedback was negative and some positive. Basically people liked Joe—as he was a likeable person—but they clearly did not like his behaviour. They validated Joe as a human being; but his behaviour was not acceptable to them. The teacher felt that this mixture of both positive and negative feedback was essential—for Joe to hear that *he* was liked and that his *behaviour* wasn't.

Joe's behaviour from that moment on changed dramatically. Out of that conversation he had the opportunity to make a choice; he recognized his need for attention (which was a big insight for him and he had been previously unaware of it) and he found that he didn't need to play the fool any more. His behaviour remained consistently different.

This opportunity led to a further sharing by Joe of a past trauma that he had been unable to share with anyone. He had found his elder brother dead in his bed some years ago and this had deeply upset him. There was some mystery around this brother's death that was never resolved and no one had bothered to help Joe come to terms with the experience. Underneath this extraordinary behaviour was a deeply distressed child, and his teacher was later able to arrange for some professional help for Joe regarding his traumatic experience.

The knowledge of 'how' to express a feeling lies within the young person himself. We need simply to ask, to probe for the meaning of the feeling and to offer the space for it to be known. The child can be shown that there are alternative ways for communication to happen, ways ranging from inappropriate physical assertion to quiet but clear communication. The child can be guided to experience how inappropriate expression is ineffective and how it might have otherwise been handled. He needs to be reinforced when he successfully communicates. Children learn by doing, and it is no loss of time for the educator to spend a few moments evoking and facilitating expression of feeling.

An example of inappropriate expression came from a class of fourteen-year-olds where one boy was being very loud and belligerent during a teacher's lecture. Another boy, who actually was interested in what the teacher was saying and wanted to work, became furiously angry, turned to the loud boy, and shouted aggressively, 'Shut up or I'll shut you up.' The loud boy said equally aggressively, 'Oh yeah, you just try', and put his clenched fists forward. The situation was escalating and the teacher knew she must intervene immediately. Rather than addressing herself to the loud boy, she spoke to the one who wanted to work and who had yelled 'shut up'— something which surprised both boys. She asked the boy if his equally aggressive command had been effective in getting him what he wanted. He realized it indeed had not and in fact was moving the situation further away from what he actually wanted. He also realized that if he got into a physical fight with this loud boy, he himself would end up the loser by getting into trouble himself. Through the teacher evoking his awareness of the consequences of his behaviour, as well as its ineffectiveness, he saw for himself that his behaviour had been inappropriate. He discovered this for himself, she did not have to tell him this truth. He also saw that there were alternative ways to get the loud boy quiet which might have been more successful, that the 'fight it out' mentality rarely worked. In this instance *he* decided that he wanted his mind to rule his feelings and that *he* needed to learn to control his own aggression and give more space to others. Interestingly enough this also led to a class discussion on behaviour in the classroom and of how *they* as a group wanted to operate.

Another method of dealing with inappropriate expression of feelings is given by one of our psychosynthesis-trained teachers:

> It often comes up with children who are failing in reading, maths or some major subject. . . . They feel very anxious, confused, and often fail themselves by making no attempt. These children are sometimes *naughty,* talkative, mess around disturbing other children *or* are very withdrawn and uncommunicative. I usually get the child to look at how he feels about his work and *failure*, bringing it into the open as gently as possible. I usually do this first with just the two of us together; then with his permission, with the whole class to enlist their support.
>
> This seems to open up a reserve of energy, and the child is frequently prepared to make a new start with his school work. He feels excited and expectant and seems to feel he has a chance. Previously he had been trying to hide it from both himself and the class—the fact that he was failing, felt a failure, scared and no good, all the while

knowing that really everyone knew. It is as if a great pressure is lifted and all that energy is now available for work.

Typically repressive attitudes in this situation would be:

1. To reinforce failure through giving inappropriate work, moaning at the child for his failures, and failing to recognize the child's feelings of pain and fear.
2. To reinforce failure by separating that child from the class, making him different, excluding him—demonstrating low expectations and little interest.
3. Making that child into the class clown so that his feelings will be repressed and covered by his *silliness*. No one sees the child.

The message that these children get is that they are failures, stupid, naughty, lazy and a *problem*. No hope.

Containment of Feelings

As previously mentioned, it is not always appropriate for the feeling that a child is experiencing to be expressed. These moments leave us with quite a dilemma. How can we encourage a feeling to be seen and known without also endorsing its expression? There is obviously a delicate line between containing a feeling and repressing it. Sometimes simply becoming aware of a feeling, and acknowledging its existence, already releases its emotive charge, enabling it to dissipate. For a child to 'know' that he has been seen and heard may provide the necessary support, so that the feeling no longer requires additional attention.

Alternatively it may be that the feeling persists and needs to be dealt with at a later and more appropriate moment. An interesting phenomenon of human experience is that, once reassured of later attention, a feeling will relax its domination of our consciousness. Giving attention later may take the form of using transformation techniques from the following section.

Ample examples of this principle arise both in the classroom or at home. The class may be engaged in some structured activity and it is not appropriate to stop that to give an individual child time to express what he is feeling. For the good of the whole, in this case the class, the child must contain his feeling. A parent is just leaving for a scheduled appointment and his child wants him to stop and listen to his feelings about something that happened at school that day—his father tells him he appreciates that it is important, acknowledges his child's feelings *and* agrees to listen later, after his appointment. The child has to contain his feelings until the appropriate moment comes. What is important here is that the *later attention* does in reality happen and the child's feelings are given time and space. This process is enhanced if the child is educated to monitor his feelings so that he can include and acknowledge them.

A natural result of containing or letting a feeling be is distancing. Distancing requires enlarging the picture psychologically to create an overall awareness:

1) that this feeling too shall pass (as all feelings do),
2) that there is not only this feeling but other feelings and other things going on within one's inner world,
3) that other people have their feelings and inner world as well, which need to be included in our perception. This essentially means creating a healthy sense of proportion, which is especially important for adolescents who tend to take themselves overly seriously. The key to keeping our feelings in proper perspective lies in our ability to bring fresh eyes and a clear outlook to each situation.

Finally, it is an undeniable fact that life is not perfect and that sometimes we must learn to live with what is. That is to say, that we must learn to accept simply that a feeling is so, allow it to be so and let it be. For the growing child this can be a hard but important lesson to learn and it requires our compassionate support and understanding.

For an example of this kind of situation, where there is nothing that can be done but learn the lesson of accepting that a feeling exists, I want to turn to a family problem. The child of a woman I was working with was experiencing great difficulty with her parents' divorce. The divorce was a reality that could not be changed. The mother had previously tried to hide her own feelings about the divorce in order to protect the child. She had done so with great difficulty and by pretending that she herself did not have some of the feelings she had.

The result was an inauthentic environment for the child, lacking a sense of reality, and with strong painful unexpressed undercurrents.

One day, the mother decided she could no longer maintain the pretence. She quietly told her daughter about the feelings she had. Her daughter was relieved that the truth was finally out but sad about the news. With her mother's support and understanding of her feelings, the child was able to accept the reality of her parents' divorce, allow herself both to have and to contain her sad feelings about it, with the recognition that this was the way it was. She had to *hold* this reality, there was no way for it to be different. There was no alternative for both the child and parent but to tell the truth. Acceptance could only be achieved through compassionate support and understanding.

A psychosynthesis-trained teacher gave me a similar example from her classroom experience:

> Children often appear in school sad or angry when their parents have split up. This happened last year. Garry suddenly burst out in class saying, 'My dad's gone and my mum's crying all the time.' We talked about it, how he thought his mother felt and how he felt. The class took an active part. Many could identify with Garry and the situation. At the end of the discussion there was, of course, no solution. I communicated to Garry that we were all here if he needed to talk about it, particularly with those who had been in the same place as him. Two twins in the class who had lost their father two weeks previously said they wanted to say something of how it had been for them . . . Lucia said it was very sad for her and still was . . . Richard said it was boring without a dad . . . Upon reflection I realized that I had used the class to support Garry in his pain giving him a way to *contain* and live with the reality of his life. . . . All the teachers I know would have said something like: 'Oh dear, what a shame' and cut it off very quickly. They wouldn't want to hear, feeling that it wasn't any of their business. They also often have an attitude that it is dangerous for children to wallow in their feelings. The problem with this is that Garry would have been left alone with his disturbance *and* it would have blocked him from being present for the activities of the class's work. We did not solve his problem; but he

clearly saw that he was not alone and that others have had similar experiences.

A less dramatic and more common experience of learning to accept the inevitable is given by the same teacher:

> It sometimes happens that I have gone through a whole series of interpersonal work with two or more children who are not friends and have had a fight. At the end one child says, 'I don't want to be friends with this person any more.' The other says, 'I want to be friends and make up.' There is nothing to be done. So I explain that this sometimes happens and we can't always have things as we may want them. I ask him how he feels at leaving it. He says sad, etc. So I say something like . . . I can see you're sad, we all can. I ask what he wants to do or what we can do for him. Depending on the reply . . . I might say OK we'll talk about it in a few days or let's see how things turn out, etc.

Transformation of Feelings

At times we may find that neither direct expression nor the containment of our feelings is possible. This is especially true for feelings of a strong and distressing nature like anger or fear. Attention feeds on itself. It is possible for a feeling to lose its grip if attention is withdrawn. To redirect attention consciously from one particular emotional experience to some other activity, and act independently of it, can not only lessen the intensity of the emotion but also transform its nature. This is a different process than inhibition by repression or negation. The difference is that inhibition by repression or negation creates an inner tension and stress between what is felt and the inhibitory reaction, whereas transformation through the redirection of energy supersedes the feeling which it inhibits and the latter vanishes or dramatically changes.

Basically, we can transform something by psychophysical release, for example, strong feelings through active play and physical discharge, or through distracting the attention, deviating it by focusing elsewhere. These tactics work especially well with feelings of anger and aggression. A younger child should have the opportunity to punch a pillow, stamp out, or exert himself physically to release these energies.

This is cathartic and can immediately help him to be liberated from the grip of his anger.

Since emotions always have a physical counterpart, we are able to give children practical ways of physically releasing their feelings. This is not meant to dispense with other forms of expression, like direct communication with the person involved, or helping a child to understand what anger is and what makes him angry. At times, especially when his anger is out of proportion or when direct expression is not appropriate, a child may need to transform—in a healthy and constructive way—these energies which would otherwise be turned against himself. It is not the feelings themselves but what we *do* with them, whether we can accept them or not, and how we express them, that determines our psychological health.

A mother once shared with me how she had dealt with her son's aggressiveness towards his sister. The boy was ten, his sister seven. From time to time the boy would be full of pent-up energy; perhaps he had had a boring day or things had not gone well at school, or he was angry with a friend. His intense feelings were not always about anything in particular, but rather the result of unchannelled energy. The problem was that his sister would end up as the target of these unused energies. When these moments came up the mother taught her son to use a large cushion instead of his sister, and to punch or beat the pillow until he no longer felt the feelings. For a period of time the family had a 'do it to a cushion instead of to each other' agreement, which both children found much safer than their previous behaviour.

Another way of coping with a younger child's feelings, especially ones of fear and anxiety, is to dissolve them and take away their power. With one group of children we talked about their fears. Each child had his own particular fear; for a few it was an authority figure, for others it was less defined and called their 'bogeyman', and for some it was a forthcoming event, like a trip to the dentist. We worked with these fears by imagining that whatever it was they feared was on the ceiling, and made friends with it. The children talked to whatever was on the ceiling, let it talk back to them, moved away or towards it; and eventually they were guided to sing a song to it which resulted in a dissolution of their feelings and turned it into something fun and playful.

Children may have certain feelings that are so strong and distressing, they don't know what to do. We need to learn how to help them come to terms with such feelings through making friends with them, dissolving them, transforming them, or directing their attention away from them.

With adolescents a more purposeful, sustained and continuous activity is appropriate and necessary for the transformation of feelings. An obvious example of this is sport—where strong feelings are directed into physical expression in a structured and coherent environment. This focused expression is what William James, the American educational philosopher, has called 'the moral equivalent of war'.[2]

William James urged that the aggressive feelings of young people should be transformed into some civic work which would be useful for society. I would agree, but perhaps qualify his 'should' to a 'could'. His idea is based on what he calls the 'expulsive power of positive emotions, thoughts and action'. If an adolescent has bad feelings or gloomy thoughts, and he can succeed in directing his attention to something interesting, positive and worthwhile, this can generate a new energy that expels or transforms the earlier feelings. To quote Dr Assagioli on this subject of transformation:

> The age of puberty (eight through fourteen) has been termed the ungrateful age. It is marked by acts if not words which represent the first 'declaration of independence'. Children rebel against the authority of parents and teachers; and their need to actively discharge their energies prompts them to combative and aggressive behaviour. *But* if aptly guided, they can display the positive qualities of this age—courage, a spirit of adventure, the capacity to endure physical hardship—and develop the feelings of comradeship and cooperation through team activities.[3]

Sublimation

The highest form of this kind of transformational work, which is only appropriate for adolescents and adults, is called sublimation. Sublimation is similar to the above technique but focuses explicitly upon a meaningful and worthwhile *ideal*. Adolescents are easily in touch with ideals, with a sense of the value and meaning of ideals, sometimes to the extreme point of being accused of lacking reality and not keeping 'their feet on the ground'. To adults, it is not fashionable to be too idealistic lest we be thought a fool. So we dare not dream, we might lose our credibility. This popular attitude towards ideals is perhaps grounded in some truth. Again to quote William James:

> The more ideals a man has, the more contemptible, on the whole, do you continue to deem him, if the matter ends there for him, and if none of the labouring man's virtues are *called into action* on his part—no courage shown, no privations undergone, no dirt or scars contracted in the attempt to get them realised. It is quite obvious that something more than the mere possession of ideals is required to make a life significant. . . .[4]

Many adolescents have the needed ideals but often lack the personality ingredients necessary to actualize those ideals, and this is where they need our support and guidance. Education enlarges our horizon and perspective, it increases the possibility of having ideals and it also can provide the resources needed to realize them. As educators we can enquire about commonly held ideals among our adolescents, mobilize their energy to direct themselves to their expression, and thereby transform the energy of their strong, passionate and sometimes inappropriate feelings.

How can we work with and evoke a realistic and healthy idealism which can both inspire our young and transform negative energies? Here are some examples taken from teachers who work with a psychosynthesis perspective. In all the following examples, the students were between twelve and seventeen years old.

One teacher brought to the class biographical articles on people who had embodied and expressed great ideals of humanity, like Gandhi, Albert Schweitzer and Martin Luther King. They would first read the articles and follow with a discussion in which altruism was discussed. How did they feel about helping others? What was the meaning of altruism? What were the qualities that these great men embodied? How did they experience and express altruism in their lives?

Following this discussion, the students talked about

people in their own lives that they also admired and why. They chose the qualities that they most admired and examined those qualities in the context of their own life: would they like to have more of them in their life? How? What form would they like these qualities to take and what stopped them from expressing those qualities right now? Practical means were explored for actualizing the qualities in their life and follow-up work was done.

Another example of this kind of work is shown by a group of young people who sang in the school choir. They themselves decided to take their music into prisons because they felt it was needed there and into homes for handicapped children because they wanted to help kids like themselves.

Another group of adolescents felt especially concerned about ecology and the environment and their own school was in a deprived area which was aesthetically horrific. They got permission to renovate a derelict lot near the school and within a few months the lot was transformed into a playground and garden for the local people.

A class of older adolescents found themselves to be especially depressed and frustrated about current social problems of racism and Third World poverty. They organized a series of lectures on these subjects, which were given outside school hours by leading authorities in the fields. The lectures were well attended by most of the school and this led to many of the students doing volunteer work with local organizations.

A particularly innovative drama class found out that nearby was a home for mentally and physically handicapped children, many of whom had speech difficulties, some of whom were not able to speak at all. The class chose to go into the home and work with a speech therapist, with musical instruments and singing to help the handicapped find a way to communicate. The process also involved physical touch, hand holding and body communication with the handicapped children. This experience was deeply moving to many of the class-members. It was difficult as well, but they reported strong feelings of having made a contribution to these handicapped children and a sense of meaning that resulted from it.

On summary then, most educators find that there are two types of emotional disturbances in the classroom: those that are 'situational', that occur spontaneously and are easily resolved; and those which are deeper, chronic, and due to larger psychological problems in the child's life. Obviously the latter are not so readily dealt with and may require more time and more therapeutic skill than an educator needs to have. Here it is wise to know one's limitations and when necessary to refer the child to a school counsellor. The suggestions for working with emotions in the previous pages do not require therapeutic training, and they may not be adequate for dealing with deeper problems.

The Mind

Healthy feelings need a healthy mind in order to be whole. There are several psychological dangers which can result from not having good mental development:

— low self-esteem and a sense of inferiority;
— low achievement in school which limits movement forward in life;
— a lack of interest in life and little curiosity, which ultimately means less choices in terms of action and involvement;
— more dependence upon other people for judgement and discrimination, having to rely on other people's options leading to less autonomy for decision-making;
— prejudice, which is an inability to look at things by transcending one's emotions and desires. This is a neurosis of the mind, a major scourge of our culture, bringing racism, prejudices towards social classes, lifestyles and other societal differences. It is a tendency to put things simplistically into boxes and an inability to awaken to the infinite 'newness' of any experience;
— inertia and lack of initiative in life. If we cannot envisage new possibilities, opportunities, alternatives we fall prey to our own habits and we stop growing.

On the other hand, a healthy mind brings with it many joys and advantages:
— the capacity to think clearly, to reflect and to concentrate deeply on a chosen area of exploration. The importance of this capability for learning is undeniable;
— the quality of openness and the possibility of not using the mind in a defensive way or in a way that limits or stops the depth of experience;

— the capacity to redirect attention, to focus, to choose where to direct the mind's energy according to what is appropriate in the situation, and to be fully present as opposed to being distracted, or being the slave of repetitive thoughts;
— creativity, the ability to express the new and to move beyond habitual grooves and patterns of thinking.

The mental exercises in this book are designed to facilitate the qualities of a healthy mind.

Head and heart duality
The mind emerges as the predominant function during adolescence or sometimes earlier. It competes with the feelings for attention. On a subconscious level the relationship between mind and feelings is being worked out. This process is complicated by the fact that feelings are so intense. There may be conflicts between the feelings themselves as well as the conflict between the feelings and the mind. Personal evolution would be much easier if the body and the feelings were to co-operate with the emergence of the mind, but often they do not.

The structure that has been created between the body and the feelings is a powerful complex. The mind, at first, is in service of the feelings and gradually moves towards developing independently and perhaps attempting to create a shift in identity; but the feelings may strongly resist. This is the classic duality between mind and feelings, or more eloquently stated, between head and heart, logos and eros. It is interesting to note that philosophers throughout the ages have commented on this duality. Of course, the mind has been developing all along, but at some point the realm of ideas, opinions, beliefs and ways of viewing the world, and even philosophical thought, become particularly active. Rather than perceiving the world from an emotional perspective of how one 'feels' about life, there is a shift to what one thinks about it.

With the awakening mental focus an interest often develops in rationality, in critical analysis and in objectivity. This is sometimes accompanied by the rejection of a more feeling-connected life, a repression of the sublime. Whereas perhaps a few years earlier a youngster was being confirmed in church, he may stop going to church and become very rational, reading about existentialism and philosophy generally. There is a decided pull towards the mind.

This conflict in adolescence has a tendency to resolve itself in one way or another, either to mind or to feelings, to head or to heart. A young person tends to choose one modality and unconsciously repress the other. Our culture supports this split in a variety of ways: for example, girls are implicitly encouraged to suppress their mind and enhance their inner relational, intuitive feeling aspect; boys, on the other hand, are supported in repressing their feeling intuitive side to become tough, rational, objective and control-orientated. Educators too reinforce this dichotomy. As Dr George Brown, director of the Department of Confluent Education, University of California, tells us:

> A grand illusion of the educational pedants has been that the exclusively rational way of knowing has been *THE* way. Rational objective thinking is what will resolve this and any other significant problem . . . What should be obvious, being continually in front of our noses, is that our thinking processes are affected in degree or kind by our feelings. . . . The emotions have something to do with the quality and quantity of our thinking . . .
>
> We can use our minds and feelings in collaboration rather than in conflict. We have a mind. And we have feelings. Why can't they both be available for harmonious engagement by us? How wasteful to turn these gifts against one another. And how tragic that through our well-meaning efforts we teach children in ways that create mind-feeling conflicts. The more we confuse control of behavior with denial or distortion of feeling, the more we subtract portions of our children's humanness.[5]

A strong psychological identification develops around either aspect, which can later be defined as being emotionally-identified or mentally-identified. This means that one modality becomes habitually the mode of operation to the exclusion of the other. There is a way of being that is associated with the mind and another way of being associated with the feelings. If I am an emotional person I behave in a certain way; or if I am a mental person I act differently. Adolescents may therefore experience an identity struggle: am I a rational thinking person or am I a passionate feeling person? Do I live from my feelings or do I live from my mind? We may encounter the academic intellectual who denies both the feelings and the body, living totally from his mind. The opposite extreme is the girl who suppresses academic ability to live out the 'inferior' female role. Many women remember how, in earlier school years, they pretended they were not as intelligent as they were or how they even consciously held back academically in order to be acceptable to their peers.

From a more mentally-identified person we might hear statements like: 'Feelings are messy, they get in the way, they confuse me and cloud my vision.' Conversely, the feeling type may say: 'The mind is cold, calculating, lacking in compassion and produces nothing but superficialities.' When feelings dominate they tell the mind what to look at, what to perceive and the mind unwittingly serves the feelings, producing 'selective perception'. When the mind dominates there is a lack of depth and quality which the feelings add to our experience and perception. The imbalance between mind and feelings remains a concern for many adults who have unconsciously repressed one function at the expense of psychological wholeness.

Mental development
Mental development is not merely a matter of an increased *amount* of mental activity. It is a *qualitative* change or refinement of the use of the mind. The various activities and uses of the mind may be summarized as follows:

1. The first function of the mind is to synthesize the sense impressions that provide the individual with an objective intelligent experience of the outer world. It may be regarded as an additional sense, co-ordinating and interpreting the messages transmitted by the other senses. It takes a detached and impersonal view. For our purposes, this function is accomplished quite well organically, although many of the suggested exercises improve and contribute to this ability.
2. The second function is to assimilate information or knowledge, to use the intellect or 'concrete' mind. It is what is commonly called reason, rationality and logic. This is

accomplished through study as we commonly know it and is already defined simply as learning. This has been an aim of teachers in the past and is still a vital function.

3. The third and somewhat higher type of mental activity is that which elaborates the material gathered in the two preced:ng ways, systemizes it, draws conclusions from it and then applies it. This is actually thinking or reflecting in the more abstract sense. This may be called the development of the abstract mind or higher mind. Herein lies the ability to abstract inner experiences into outer realities, as well as seeing patterns and wholes.

4. The fourth and a later developing function of the mind is that of becoming receptive to the intuition, understanding and interpreting it correctly. The primary focus of this experiential section will be on the development of the abstract mind, and many techniques for working with the Transpersonal also encourage it.

In the East the symbol of the lotus is viewed as representing the evolution of the personality. With the lotus, the roots are in the mud (earth) symbolizing the physical body. The stem is in the water, embodying feelings which grow from the body. The flower of the lotus (mind) is in the air, although resting in the water and connected with the stem (feelings). The perfume floats upward from the flower representing the spirit, being open to the air as well as contributing to it.

EXERCISES

YOU AND YOUR BODY

Knowing our body is basic to knowing ourselves. The more in touch with and conscious of his body an individual is, the greater his experience of aliveness. Increased body awareness may also bring increased physical health. This exercise helps to focus attention on all parts of the body, and enables the participant to learn to relax. It is an effective way to introduce lessons on health and hygiene or can be used with the following exercise LISTENING TO YOUR BODY.

Age: seven–adult
Time: 30 minutes for exercise
       20 minutes for processing the experience

Exercise:

Find a partner. Each partner choose 'A' and 'B'.

'A' lies on the floor, 'B' sits beside him and watches.

All 'A's close your eyes and breathe slowly and deeply.

Breathing slowly and deeply draw your breath down to reach into your toes and feet.

Next let your breath move along your legs . . .

Now feel your breath fill the whole area of your bottom . . .

Let your breathe move into your stomach . . .

Fill out your chest with breath . . .

Draw your breath down into your fingers and hands, your arms, your neck and feel it in your face.

Fill the inside of your head with your breath.

Continue breathing normally and allow the floor to support your body totally.

Focus your attention as completely as possible on your body.

Let your body be just as it is, without changing anything.

Notice how it feels inside your body . . . how it feels outside.

What is a body?

Your partner is going to lift different parts of your body. Do not help or hinder. Do not control or resist your limbs from being lifted.

Just allow yourself to be a very limp body, like a rag doll.

Focus your attention totally on the area that is being lifted. Listen to it. What does it feel like? Do some parts feel different to others?

Now all 'B's move into a comfortable position nearest your partner's arm. Very gently and carefully slide your hand underneath his arm and very very slowly and sensitively begin to lift it. Explore the different ways this arm can move. You can lift it quite high, but gently.

Now put the arm down and move to a leg. (Allow time for each limb and finally the head, instructing when to change and move on.) Lift *all* the limbs.

Now those of you lying, very slowly begin to wiggle your toes and your fingers, then your hands and feet, legs and arms and sit up, then stand.

When ready change partners. (Guide the second group through the same process as above.)

The whole group stands up. Move around the room now using all your limbs, feeling your legs, your arms, your head moving. Move slowly with your limbs. Move quickly with them.

Processing the experience:
Form a circle, sit down and let's share your experience. What did your body tell you? How does it move? What does your body do for you?

Alternatively, this exercise can be immediately followed by the LISTENING TO YOUR BODY exercise.

LISTENING TO YOUR BODY

This exercise is designed to give a basic assessment of the participant's relationship with his body, as well as his feelings and attitude towards it. It first brings awareness of what is true at the moment with one's body and subsequently explores what can be done to improve our relationship with it. It uses the imagination as a means of communicating with the body in order to increase recognition, acceptance and understanding of the body's needs—both objectively and psychologically.

Age: seven–adult
Time: 30 minutes for the exercise
   30 minutes for processing the experience
Equipment: A sheet of paper and crayons for each participant.
Exercise:
Find a space and lie down. Relax and breathe deeply a few times. Feel your body on the floor, make yourself comfortable.

Our bodies can talk to us, to tell us things we need to know. Do you know how your body talks to you? How do you know when to eat, drink or sleep, or put on more clothes? We usually listen to our bodies, but not always. Sometimes we don't know how to listen, how to hear what our body is trying to tell us. Right now we are going to find a new way to talk and listen to our bodies.

Breathe in and out deeply several times, letting go of any tension that you are aware of. Become aware of your whole body. How does your body feel right now?

In a moment you will see an image or a picture in your imagination that represents your body. It might look like your real body or it might be something that symbolizes or reminds you of your body, like a flower or a machine. It can be anything that you see inside your mind that seems to be connected with your body.

When you see this image or picture let it become vivid and clear so that you can see it well. If it is not too clear, you can ask it to become clearer and it will. The image or picture will communicate something about your body to you.

Let's imagine that this image or picture that you see can talk to you about your body. It speaks as your body. What does it have to say? It probably has something to tell you. Listen for a moment and let it speak to you. It may tell you about how it feels or what it is like to be a body.

Listen with your inner ear to hear what the image is saying. You may even want to answer it back and have a real conversation. Maybe it needs something that you are not giving it right now. Find out if your body needs anything.

See if you can make friends with this image in your imagination. Get to know each other better. Find out what your body does for you. (Guide should spend as much time with this section as feels appropriate, according to the attention span of participants.)

When you have finished the conversation with your image, say goodbye. When you are ready, open your eyes, quietly begin to draw the picture you saw in your imagination or your sense or feeling about your body. It does not need to look like your real body. It's like something that reminds you of your body.

Processing the experience:
When you have finished make small groups of three or four and show your drawings for your body and share your experience, focusing on how you can listen better to your body and take better care of it.

HANDS ARE . . .

This exercise focuses upon the hands, but may be used for any body part, like feet, arms, legs or head, as a means of exploration. It both increases observation and concentration skills and heightens awareness of the various functions of the body part. It can enable the participants to learn to appreciate what their body does for them.
Age: seven–fourteen

Time: 30 minutes for exercise

   15 minutes for processing the experience

Equipment: Crayons, pencil and one sheet of paper per participant.

Exercise:

Find a partner. Choose who is going to start.

Look at your partner's hands, both sides. Look at the colour, the lines. Are your partner's hands long or short, thin or plump? Are there any interesting marks on them? Gently feel them all over. How do they feel?

   Now tell your partner what you found out about their hands. (Repeat the process with the other partner.)

   Now look at your own hands in the same way.

(Guide participants through the above process with their own hands.)

   Everyone close their eyes and become very quiet. See yourself in your imagination using your hands. Remember all the things your hands can do. All the actions, all the jobs, kind things and unkind, interesting and boring, difficult and easy. Now open your eyes and see if you can finish this sentence: 'My hands are _____.' (Write the incomplete statement on the board.) Fill in the sentence two or three times and write it down.

   On your piece of paper, take a pencil and draw round your hands. Make sure you leave enough room for the second hand.

Underneath your hands write your sentence or sentences.

My hands are _____.

   Now decorate your hands so that the decoration goes with the sentence(s). If you have writen two very different sentences, you may want to decorate each hand differently.

Processing the experience:

Share with your partner your drawing and sentence(s).

How do you feel about your hands? Do you appreciate them or not? What do you like about them? Dislike? What do your hands do for you? What would it be like not to have them?

   The hand drawings can be displayed and shared in the large group as well.

THIS IS YOUR BODY

This drawing exercise will encourage the participant to become aware of how he feels about his body, what he likes and what he dislikes. It will enable communication about problems and what may be done about them. Its purpose is to increase body awareness, improve body health, help the participant to come to terms with his body image and how he presents himself to the world.

Age: seven–fourteen
Time: 30 minutes for exercise
one hour for processing the experience
Equipment: Large long sheets of paper, scissors, crayons and pencils.
Exercise:

Choose a partner. One of you lie down on your sheet of paper with arms out and legs apart. Hold the pencil straight up and keep it gently touching your partner as you trace around their body outline. Be careful to get the fingers, neck, hair and shoes on the paper.

Switch and repeat step one for your partner.

Cut out your body outlines.

Now colour and fill in your body cut-out without thinking too much about it, using any colours that you feel inclined to use. Let the colouring also express how you feel about the various parts of your body. It does not have to show how you are dressed right now nor must it be totally realistic. You are colouring in your feelings and spontaneous sense of it all . . . Just let yourself be free.

Processing the experience:
Upon completion the body cut-outs can be put on the wall and each person given time to talk about their body, how it feels to see it on the wall and how they feel about any places on the drawing that require attention. If the group is large it can be broken down into smaller groups with an adult facilitating the sharing.

DEEP RELAXATION

Learning to relax the body consciously is an essential skill for confronting any anxiety-producing life experience. It can help to overcome excessive fear and stress before an examination, or any performance or activity which demands skilful behaviour. Since we cannot be tense and relaxed at the same time, wasting energy through muscle tension is unnecessary. By choosing to practise deep muscle relaxation it is possible to displace apprehension.

Ages: seven–adult

Time: 15 minutes

Exercise:

Let's begin by lying on our backs on the floor and not touching anyone else. Wiggle around a little until you find a way of lying down that is completely comfortable. Now close your eyes and think of your hands. Feel the bones inside them, feel the muscles that move the bones, feel the weight of them on the floor. Now make a fist with your hands and clench tightly. Hold your hands tightly (ten seconds). Now relax and feel the soothing, tingling feeling of relaxation come into your hands. (Pause ten seconds or so between instructions.)

Now draw up your arms and tighten your biceps as tight as you can. Hold them tightly. (Ten seconds.) Now relax and feel the tension drain out of your arms.

Shrug your shoulders now, pushing them as if to push them up through your arm. Hold them there tightly (ten seconds). Now let them go and feel all the tension drain out of your body.

Continuing to keep your eyes closed, open your mouth as far as it will go, stretching the muscles at the corners of your mouth. Hold it tightly (ten seconds). Now let go and relax. Let the peaceful feeling of relaxation flow through your body.

Now press your tongue against the roof of your mouth and tighten your jaw muscles. Press tightly and hold it (ten seconds). Now let go and relax. Let the peaceful feeling of relaxation flow through your body.

Now wrinkle your nose and make a face. Scrunch up your face tightly and hold it (ten seconds). Relax now, feeling the tension flow out of your face.

Now tighten the muscles of your chest, stomach and abdomen. Draw all the muscles in tightly and hold them tense (ten seconds). Now let them go, feeling the soothing feeling of relaxation pour in.

Now tense the muscles of your thighs by straightening your legs. Hold them tightly (ten seconds). Now relax your thighs—let all the tension drain out of them.

Now tense the backs of your legs by straightening your feet. Hold your legs tensely (ten seconds). Now relax them and let all of the tension go.

Now tense your feet by curling your toes. Keep them curled tightly (ten seconds). Now relax your toes and feel the delicious feeling of relaxation come to your feet.

Your whole body is feeling loose and relaxed now. Feel yourself completely supported on the floor, and breathe deeply; as you breathe in, let each breath fill your body with deeper and deeper feelings of relaxation.

See if there are any places of tension left in your body. If you feel tense in some area, take a deep breath and send the breath to that place. Fill that tense area with breath, and let the feeling of tension leave your body.

Let the soothing feeling of relaxation fill your body. Each breath takes you deeper and deeper into relaxation. (Pause thirty seconds.)

Now you will be coming out of relaxation in a moment, and you will feel rested and alert. I will count backward from ten to one, and as I do feel your body becoming alert at your own rate.

Ten, nine, eight, feel the alertness returning to your body. Seven, six, five, feel your toes and fingers begin to move. Four, three, move your arms and legs. Two, eyes. One, get up slowly, feeling completely rested and alert.

Note: Although there are many versions of this exercise, the most effective one I've found is from: Gay Hendricks and Russell Wills, *The Centering Book,* p. 41.

THE FIVE SENSES

Full sensory experience enriches sensitivity and enhances the depth of life, leading to more active participation, learning and body awareness. The degree to which all five senses are awake and alert influences the amount of pleasure derived from educational work. This exercise helps to heighten and refine sensory awareness.

Ages: seven–twelve
Time: 45 minutes for the exercise
    30 minutes for processing the experience
Equipment: One piece of crisp fruit or vegetable (apple or carrot).

Exercise:

Sit comfortably with a partner. Close your eyes and take a few deep breaths. Relax your whole body. Still keeping your eyes closed, put your hand forward and wait until you receive an object. Without opening your eyes, use your hands and fingers to tell you what the object is, its shape and every detail about it. Explore and learn about your object by touching it.

Now open your eyes and share with your partner what it was like for you to explore this object with the sense of *touch*.

Now take your object in your hands and smell it all over. Does it smell the same everywhere or do some parts smell differently? What kind of smell is it—sweet, sour, strong or weak? Really get to know your object by its smell.

Put your object down and again share with your partner what it was like to use your sense of *smell*.

Pick up your object again. Look at it closely. What do your eyes tell you about it? Its shape, its size, its colours, its marks or anything else that is special about it . . . How many different things can you notice about the way it looks?

When you have really *seen* your object, put it down. Share with your partner your experience of *seeing*, of what your eyes actually do for you.

Close your eyes and take a bite of your object. Slowly begin to chew and bite it—but very slowly. What does it sound like when you chew slowly? What can you taste? Is it sweet or bitter? What texture is it? Do you like its taste?

Put your object down and open your eyes. Now share with your partner what you experienced with the sense of *taste*. How was it for you? Do you normally fully taste what you eat?

Processing the experience:

Bring the group together. Have a discussion on the senses. What is their value and use? How do they serve us? What is their importance? Which senses felt most familiar? Strange? Comfortable? What did you learn from this experience? Would you like to use your senses more? Why? How can you do that?

EXPLORING WITHOUT SEEING

This experience heightens awareness of the senses, bringing

the participant into a feeling experience through the body. It is particularly useful for the integration of body and feelings. It also facilitates the participant's ability to trust others. It should not be done until the participants know each other and are comfortable wearing a blindfold for at least five minutes.

Age: ten–adult
Time: 10–30 minutes for exercise
     15 minutes for processing the experience
Equipment: This exercise can be done indoors or outdoors; although outdoors is recommended. The environment should be safe and somehow limited in space. A blindfold for every group of two children is required.
Exercise:
Choose a partner, someone you feel comfortable with.
One of you will put on the blindfold, whilst the other will direct and do the 'seeing' for both of you. *Neither of you should talk at all or make sounds,* during this exercise.

The seeing partner: Take your partner for a walk, after adjusting the blindfold, and provide as many experiences as possible, starting with:

Guiding your partner to a tree, to touch the bark.

Suggest putting his arms around the trunk, to experience the nature of the tree, its size and strength.

Take your partner to a shrub and experience its shape, size, and quality.

Guide your partner to flowers and leaves, to smell, to touch, textures and shapes.

Direct your partner to a wall, to touch the different textures of bricks, mortar, cement, rocks, etc. Press his body against a wall to experience its nature and pressure and temperature.

Take your partner for a walk on grass, gravel, stones, concrete, wood, and listen to the different sounds that these textures make.

When finished, rest with your partner and see how many sounds can be heard, inside the body, and outside, near at hand and further away.

Change partners and repeat the experience.

Processing the experience:
What did you learn by your walk?

How did it feel to be led?
How did it feel to be the leader?
Did you feel scared?
Did you learn something about yourself in each role?
Did you learn something extra about your environment in
each role?
Would you like to do it again?

PREPARATION FOR A NEW SKILL

Learning a new skill can be positive and enjoyable or
traumatic. This preparatory exercise can lead to mastery
through teaching the participant to listen to his body when
learning a new physical skill and can help to integrate body
and mind through the use of the imagination. To imagine
successfully performing a new skill enlarges the potential for it
happening. Mental *rehearsals* will help the participant to
become aware of any feelings that might block or inhibit his
learning. It can be used for learning any physical skill, like
doing a forward roll, a team game, yoga, riding a bike and so
on; but it could also be applied to learning a social skill.
Age: eight–adult
Time: Determined by the skill to be learned.
Equipment: Determined by the skill to be learned.
Exercise:
Before we begin learning our new skill today, let's think about
what you are going to enjoy the most when you are learning it.
When you know, write it down. Now what are you going to
dislike the most? Write that down too. Now tell your partner
what you're going to enjoy most and dislike most.

(The educator should show participants the correct skill,
so they have a clear idea of what they are going to be doing.
Break the skill down into steps or stages.) Let's all try the first
step or stage. Allow adequate time to complete first stage.

How did your body feel when you did that first step?
What part felt strained? What part felt comfortable? Be aware
of this.

Was there any tension anywhere in your body?

Keep practising this first step for a few times. (Educator
here may move around giving help and suggestions.)

(Repeat as above for each step or stage of the new skill.)

Now find a comfortable place to sit or lie down. Close

your eyes and find a quiet place inside yourself. In your imagination see yourself successfully doing your new skill. Now see yourself doing it again and again.

Open your eyes and sit up. How many of you did it successfully in your imagination? (Here it may be necessary to have the participants working at different levels. If someone did not successfully imagine themselves doing the skill, they need to practise the steps again or spend more time visualizing.)

Everyone now do the new skill physically (as many times as is appropriate).

Processing the experience:
Break into large or small groups and talk about your experience. What happened to you? How did you feel when learning the new skill? How did you feel when visualizing the new skill? Were you afraid? What, if anything, stopped you from visualizing yourself doing the skill well? What can you do about your obstacle if there was one?

THE FEELINGS WE HAVE

This is a preparatory exercise for beginning any work with the feelings and it helps the participant to begin to focus on his emotional life. It enables feelings to be articulated and better understood in their subtleties, and increases discrimination. It also evokes the free expression and release of feelings. Words may be adapted according to the age and maturity of participants. This exercise is a recommended foreunner to GETTING TO KNOW YOUR FEELINGS.

Age: seven–adult
Time: 20 minutes
Exercise:
Let's all stand up, with enough space to swing your arms all around you. Make sure you can swing your arms without bumping into anyone.

Find a little space that is just for you. You may want to close your eyes or keep them open; whatever feels best. Stand with your feet a fair distance apart, solidly planted on the floor so that you feel stable.

Let your body begin to sway back and forth and your arms swing at your sides, and your head can move if it wants to. Allow your arms and head to move freely.

Now go inside yourself and see what it is that you are feeling right now.

What are you feeling? Happy? A little sad? Maybe tired or grumpy? Whatever you find inside that you are feeling, let your body begin to move and become like that feeling. Let your body begin to express that, almost as if you were a statue of that feeling inside. You might want to move a little bit.

Now begin to explore some of the other feelings you have had today, different ones than the ones you have now.

How did you feel when you got up this morning or at lunch-time today? Let all these other feelings that you have felt today also come out through your body, and movement. What sounds would they make? Growls, laughs?

Let some sounds come out with these feelings. In a way these feelings are still there somewhere inside you. Let all the feelings you have had today come out of you through your body and your sounds.

Now we all sometimes feel bad or negative, even though we might not like to. We sometimes feel angry, sad, irritated or resentful. These are the feelings that we don't really like to have inside us, but they get in anyway.

Let's allow all of those negative, unhappy feelings that we sometimes have, to come out of us now. Let your body express them and the sounds that go with them. In fact, exaggerate them and make them bigger and louder as you let them out.

You can shake them out with your body and with your sounds. Shake out all these feelings. When you're ready, slow down and stand quietly.

Now, look inside for feelings that you love to have. You all have many of those. What are those feelings that make you feel good, that make you smile, or laugh, or sing, or dance? Remember, all those feelings are also somewhere inside you. Those are the ones that are good to have.

Let us have fun now and let those happy, joyous feelings come out from inside through your body.

Let your body express all these pleasant feelings. Make all the sounds that go with them, laughter, joy, or whatever. When you've finished go back to your seats.

GETTING TO KNOW YOUR FEELINGS

Sometimes we are unaware of what we are feeling at any particular moment, and we don't know *how* to listen to our feelings. It is our feeling life that adds depth and aliveness to our experience. By recognizing, including and accepting feelings we can have a richer relationship with them and learn to listen to what they are telling us. Sometimes we neglect them or pretend they don't exist, at the expense of knowing who we are. The purpose of this exercise is to assess the participant's relationship with his feeling life and to explore ways to improve that relationship. It also provides a means of better understanding and integrating feelings.

Age: seven–adult

Time: 30 minutes for exercise

30 minutes for processing the experience

Equipment: Crayons and one sheet of paper for each participant.

Exercise:

Now sit or lie back with your eyes closed. Take a few deep breaths and let your body relax. How are you feeling right now? Take some time to become aware.

In a moment you will see an image or a picture in your imagination that is related to or represents your feelings. It might be a symbol that is like your feelings: for example a frog or a tree. It might not make sense to you, but whatever you see is related to your feelings and it does not have to make sense. It can be anything you see in your mind or imagination that seems to be connected to your feelings.

Whatever you see has something to tell you and to communicate to you. So listen to what the image says to you now. Let it speak to you. Find out what it has to say. If your image is not too clear you can ask it to become clearer so that you can talk to it. Remember that in your imagination anything can happen and anything can talk . . .

What is it saying to you? You can also answer it back if you want to. The two of you can have a conversation. The image for your feelings will probably tell you about how it feels. It might even want something from you or tell you it needs more love, more freedom, more laughter, more expression or whatever. Find out if your feelings want or need anything from you. Listen with your inner ear to what the image is saying . . .

You might want to tell your feelings what you want from them. Do you want them to be more happy? Or maybe you would like to be able to cry more? Or perhaps it would be nice to yell loudly sometimes . . . Try to get to know this image for your feelings better. Make friends with each other. See if you can establish a better relationship. Ask your feelings what they have to give to you.

As you talk the picture in your imagination might change a bit and this is okay. (The guide should spend as much time with this section as feels appropriate, according to the participants' response.)

When you feel ready you can say goodbye to this image. Then open your eyes and begin to draw the picture you saw in your imagination or draw a picture of your feelings. It doesn't have to look just like the image you had in your mind. It can be any drawing you want that is connected with or related to your feelings. It is like drawing something that symbolizes or reminds you of your feelings.

Processing the experience:
After the participants have drawn, break them into small groups of three or four and invite them to share the experience and their drawing. Focus their discussion on how they can get along better with their feelings.

BASIC HUMAN EMOTIONS: TELLING IT LIKE IT IS

An emotional experience left unconscious and unrecognized creates repression and lack of aliveness as well as isolation. Young people have intense feelings which need to be acknowledged, accepted and sometimes transformed. It can be liberating to discover that they are not alone in their joys and struggles and that others have similar feelings. To know the basic interconnectedness of human emotion can enhance interpersonal relationships and foster communication skills. This exercise is designed to facilitate positive acceptance of feelings, and begins to introduce the possibility of choices and alternative behaviours.

Age: seven–adult
Time: one hour for exercise
       one hour for processing the experience

Equipment: At least four sheets of paper and crayons per participant.

Exercise:

Sit comfortably, close your eyes and take a few deep breaths. Remember a time in your life when you felt really happy. It might have been yesterday, or a few weeks ago, or a few years ago. In your imagination see that happy time and feel how happy you were. Let your body feel this happy memory. Remember how the situation was for you, where you were and what you were doing. Were you alone or with other people? What kind of feeling was that happy feeling? What were your thoughts in that happy moment? Let your memory of this experience come alive right now and relive it as vividly as possible.

Now open your eyes and draw that experience of a happy time in your life. Draw any part of that experience that you wish and in any way that you wish. If you could not recall a happy experience, just let your hand move on its own and draw whatever you feel like that reminds you of happy feelings. It does not need to be a picture of anything. It may just be colours and shapes or images that express these feelings for you. Let yourself express freely onto paper your perception of the feeling of happiness.

Repeat the above process of experiences of: anger, fear, sadness. Any emotion can be chosen for this process like love, unity, compassion or gratefulness.

Processing the experience:

Now you have your feelings which are a valid part of you. With a partner, or in small groups, share your drawings and experiences.

Useful questions to be explored with each drawing:

Where in your body did you feel this emotion?

With the negative feelings—what did you feel at the time was the worst thing that could happen to you?

Imagine at that time you had had a magic wand, what would you most liked to have made happen? How could you actually have made that happen?

What would you do differently if you could recreate that experience all over again?

What did that experience tell you about yourself? About life?

CYCLES OF GROWTH

This guided visualization enables participants to become aware of and to experience the evolutionary cycle of growth of which we are all a part. It uses the metaphor of a caterpillar unfolding to become a butterfly, a journey of development with which to identify. This metaphor, when experienced symbolically, stimulates a similar process in the unconscious of the participant. It helps to build a positive self-image of life and growth, implicitly demonstrating the *ups and downs*, joys and struggles of the life process.

Age: seven–twelve

Time: 20 minutes for exercise

20 minutes for processing the experience

Exercise:

Find a space. Lie down. Relax your legs, relax your arms, relax your whole body. Close your eyes and find the quiet space inside you.

Imagine that you are a tiny egg swaying on a large leaf. You are inside this egg. You cannot move at all. You are stuck.

The sun warms your skin. The rain softens it. Gradually, time passes and you begin to feel a big change. Everything inside this skin is changing. You begin to feel life, and it's a miracle.

Suddenly, you begin to move, ever so slightly at first. You begin to uncurl, you must get out, you wriggle. The skin splits and you are free. You are tiny. You have many parts which move together as one. You are a tiny caterpillar. You are certainly hungry.

You gobble everything around you. You eat and eat and eat. You learn new things. You grow bigger and bigger and bigger. Everyone sees you as a great big greedy caterpillar but all the time you carry a big secret inside you. You know that you are not really just a caterpillar but that you can also become a butterfly.

But first you have to go on a journey of transformation. So you begin to prepare. You eat and eat and store all the food inside you. You also grow a coat to protect you, a golden silk cocoon.

One day, suddenly, you stop. You don't eat any more. You just rest. The cocoon is all around you, it keeps you safe. It is like being in the womb. It is dark. It is as if you are half-awake, waiting, waiting. But just as it was in the egg, whilst you are waiting, you feel many changes going on inside you.

Feel how some parts are breaking down and dissolving. Feel how some parts are building up and growing. It feels very strange and scary, yet you know that it will be alright in the end. You have to trust.

Everything feels as if it is neatly folded together: legs, yes; wings, yes; feelers, yes; everything is in its proper place. The light, from outside, increases through the walls of your cocoon. It is getting warmer and warmer and your cocoon is uncomfortable inside. Phew! You can't really stand it much longer inside.

Crack! There is a split at the top. The light floods in. Slowly you wriggle and wriggle and wriggle. The hole gets bigger and you crawl out. The sun dries you off. The breeze suddenly lifts you up. You open your wings and off you fly. You are a butterfly and the waiting is over. You have become what you were meant to become.

You can now fly where you like, how you like and as you like. FLY! See the earth all around you. See the great fields, the flowers, the trees and all the space. It is all yours to explore, to see, to smell, to taste, to touch with many sounds to hear. What a miraculous change from the tiny egg, stuck to a leaf, to becoming and being a beautiful butterfly.

As you let the image subside, keep the lightness, the freedom, the capacity to move from one thing to another *within you*. Then slowly, when you are ready, return to the room.

Processing the experience:
Break into small groups of three or four and discuss your experiences. How did it feel to go through these stages of life? How are we humans like the caterpillar? What can this experience tell us about your life?

TRANSFORMING A NEGATIVE FEELING
We do not need to be victims to our negative emotions, nor do we have to blindly act them out, expressing them in destructive ways.

A problem or difficult emotion can be seen, known,

understood and transformed. Negative feelings are usually trying to tell us something, contain a meaning which is important, and often represent an unfulfilled need. To push away and try to get rid of these unwanted feelings only increases their hold on us. To work with them creatively, learn their message, understand their cause, is to liberate ourselves. This exercise provides a useful model for working with any problematic feeling. It teaches participants how to take responsibility for their emotions and empowers them to change.

Age: eight–adult
Time: 20 minutes for the exercise
      30 minutes for processing the experience
Exercise:
Find a comfortable position with eyes closed. Take a few deep breaths and slowly allow your body to relax. Breathe away any tensions or stress. Adopt, as much as you are able, an attitude of acceptance. Recognize that you have many many different feelings, some good and some difficult. Right now we will explore a difficult feeling or problem we have.

Bring into your awareness a problem or difficult feeling you consistently have with which you would like to come to terms. It can be absolutely anything. For example: a feeling of anger, or fear, or shyness, or insecurity, or grief and sadness, or aggression, or self-pity, etc. Choose one such feeling to work with right now.

Think about this difficult feeling. Remember when you experience it; what situations tend to evoke it; what people are involved with the feeling. Let yourself experience that feeling right now. Where in your body do you experience it? How is it for you? It may be painful, but as much as you are able to, let that feeling be with you right now.

Now slowly and gradually allow an image or a symbol to appear that is related to this feeling for you. It can be any kind of image. Don't censor or judge your image. Allow it to become vivid and clear.

This image or symbol has something to communicate to you; and it may be with or without words. Let it speak to you of its meaning, and about this difficulty you have. Simply be receptive to what this image has to communicate, be open to it.

Ask the image or symbol what it needs. See if you know

how to give it what it needs. Allow yourself to be present with this experience right now and allow whatever is necessary to happen. Tell the image what you need from it. Through your exchange or dialogue find a way to meet both your needs.

Ask this image how you can move through and beyond the problem. Let it answer you. It may again be with or without words. What needs to happen in relation to this difficulty you are having?

When you are ready, say goodbye to the image.

Take a few deep breaths and let go of the previous image as much as possible. Now allow another image or symbol to emerge, this time one that is related to or symbolic of what you need, within yourself, in order to move through this difficulty. Be receptive and wait for the image to emerge gradually. Accept the image without judgement. Allow it to become vivid and clear.

Now allow this image to communicate with you in some way about what you need, and about what needs to happen in order for you to go forward. What is the quality of this image? What is the message this symbol has for you? Let yourself receive its message.

When you feel ready, take as much time as you need, bring yourself back here to this room and take a few minutes to write about this experience.

Processing the experience:
Break into small groups of four people with whom you would like to share this exercise. In your sharing pay particular attention to what was needed to move through the difficulty. Group members help each other with this exploration. Look for the positive step you can take in order to resolve this difficulty.

When each group is complete, come back to the large group for any final sharing.

FINDING A GIFT
This guided imagery exercise is for younger children and can help them to discover what it is they personally need in their lives at the moment.
Age: six to thirteen

Time: 20 minutes for the exercise
         15 minutes for processing the exercise
Equipment: Crayons and one sheet of paper for each participant.
Exercise:
Be comfortable and relax. Find a quiet place inside you. Imagine that you are in a meadow. It is a beautiful day, the sun is shining, the sky is clear blue. There are flowers growing in your meadow and perhaps you can smell their fragrance. There are trees growing at the edge of this meadow. Maybe there is a stream nearby. Listen to see if you can hear the sound of water.

Begin to walk around the meadow. Enjoy being there with the sun on your face and the grass under your feet. As you walk you begin to know that you are going to find something in this meadow, somewhere. You don't know where, but you feel sure that you will. You trust that your feet will lead you to the place where you will find something that is special for you—important to you—a special and meaningful thing.

Now you become aware of where it is and you go to that place and find your special something, your gift. If you can't see anything, make something up now. Look at it very carefully. If it is something you can pick up, pick it up. If not, touch it in some way if you want to. Do whatever feels right for you to do. Spend some time with what you've found.

In some way say thank you for the gift. Slowly come back into this room and draw your experience.

Processing the experience:
Find a partner and share your experience and your drawing. What is the meaning of your gift? How can you use it in your life?

DIRECTING YOUR LIFE

Every situation or experience in life can be lived in a full and conscious way. Sometimes we are so lost or identified in a particular experience that we find ourselves *asleep*, unaware of the meaning it brings. We can be both the *actor* and the *director* of our life. Ultimately we are responsible for everything that happens to us; we can learn to take charge of our life, and learn to make choices that are consistent with *how* we would like to be.

This exercise uses creative *drama* and *play* for participants to explore some basic human experiences, which we all have to cope with and hopefully learn from, both the so-called negative and positive moments of life.

Age: eight–adult

Time: This exercise can take a varied amount of time, depending on age of participants and time available. When done in a classroom situation, it can be done over a period of days if the educator wishes each class member to have the experience. Each enactment takes about one hour.

Equipment: Each group of four has one set of three cards with the following situations written on each card.

> A. 'A situation or time when you felt misunderstood, excluded or blamed for something you felt was unfair.'
>
> B. 'A situation or time when you felt really angry with someone.'
>
> C. 'A situation or time when you felt really good about yourself, perhaps excited by something you were doing, or appreciated by someone else, a time when you were great.'

Exercise:

One person will be the director of the situation, which he chooses from card A, B, or C. He then recalls an experience from his own life which corresponds to the situation on the card. The director can choose any of the three cards, and any experience from his life. The director tells each member of his group what the experience was and who they will be playing from that experience. Group members are going to role-play this experience and it will be re-enacted. Remember one of them must pretend to be *you*, as you are the director.

You are going to be the director and will watch the actors re-enact your experience. Tell them *how* to play their parts and what to say. You also tell them how to move and behave and what they do.

Go ahead now and re-enact this situation. As director, you can intervene at any moment and make changes that you wish. You can tell whoever is playing yourself how you want them to be, what you want them to say, if you want them to act differently and so on. (Allow as much time as is appropriate for the enactments.)

Upon completion of the re-enactments, discuss with your group what happened. Did you learn anything new about that time in your life? Is there anything you would like to change if a similar situation happened again? What different choices could you have made then? What did you need in that situation?

LIFE DRAWINGS

All children love to talk about themselves and to tell the story of their life. To do this in a classroom environment gives *each* participant the opportunity to feel included, to be a recognized part of the group. Telling one's life story also fosters an awareness of the *process* of growth, the unfoldment of change and development. It also helps to bring to the foreground problem areas, and can provide a framework for future sharing and exploration.

Age: ten to adult

Time: 30 minutes–one hour (depending on age of participants) for exercise

one hour for processing the experience

Equipment: One large, long sheet of paper (three to four feet) and crayons for each participant. Water colours or tempera paint may be used.

Exercise:

We are each going to draw or paint the story of our life. It does not have to be done in any special way and is *not* an art project. Start with when you were born and draw from there. Draw your parents, any brothers or sisters you had, your family house or flat. Draw your earliest memories.

Then when you are ready draw the next parts of your life that you remember. Perhaps you remember your first school. How did you feel there? Draw your first friends and classmates. Just draw your feelings of your early childhood, happiness, fear, difficult moments, positive moments, etc. You may remember special events or situations, family relationships. Draw whatever stands out to you. Let your drawing unfold towards the present moment, including the people, events, situations and feelings that you may have a sense of.

(Educator should monitor the time according to age of participants.)

Processing the experience:
This can be done in a variety of ways.
A. Break into small groups of three to four and share the drawings. How do you feel about your life? What does your drawing tell you? What stands out to you about it? Did you forget anything? Are there any repetitious feelings or experiences that you notice?
B. For use in the classroom, following the drawings, each participant could write an autobiography or story of their life, to read to the class or as a project.
C. Put all the life stories on the wall with each participant having the opportunity to share his life with the entire class. (This is especially effective at the beginning of a school year.)

WHAT WE MAY BE

We all carry, consciously or unconsciously, a self-image or model of ourselves and of how we function and express our personality in the world. This self-image is not one model only, but a variety whose nature, origin and energy level are not only diverse but often one-sided, impractical, restrictive and in conflict with each other.

It is useful to achieve an image of ourselves, an ideal model, which is *realistic* and which we truly can become. This model is not an ultimate model of perfection but is the next step in our growth, such as strengthening some undeveloped psychological function, building latent qualities, or establishing a more effective pattern of action.

Creative imagination is a powerful tool for personal growth. It can be used to form an ideal model, thus evoking energy and direction, and eliciting outward expression. To do this we need first to recognize and understand the multiplicity of models which limit our appreciation of what we can be. Then we can proceed to the ideal model itself.

Age: fourteen years to adulthood.
Time: 45 minutes for exercise
45 minutes for processing the experience
Equipment: Five sheets of drawing paper and crayons per participant.

Exercise:

1. Close your eyes. Breathe in and out slowly. Let go of all the tension in your body. Allow your energies to subside and feel yourself relax.

All of us *under-evaluate* ourselves in some way.

We each have an image or model of ourselves *which is worse* than we really are. It is negative and exaggerated. Sometimes we believe this model to be true.

Get in touch with this model of how you under-evaluate yourself. Pay attention to what you know about it. Experience what your feelings are about it. Take some time to do this. Study it for a while.

Now get an image in your mind which can represent that experience. It can take the form of a person, a symbol, an abstract pattern or just colours. It represents and expresses this overly negative self-image.

When you are ready, open your eyes and draw a picture of that image of yourself. If you don't get an image, don't worry, you can just begin to draw and let it come. Write down your feelings of what this self-image means in your every-day life. When you have finished, number it (1) and turn it over.

Become still. Clear your mind of this experience. Take a few deep breaths and allow your body to relax. Close your eyes.

2. We also *over-evaluate* ourselves in some ways. We have within us an exaggerated overly positive self-image.

You have an image of yourself which is better than you really are. It is usually unreal and unattainable. Again think of it for a while.

Get in touch with the model of how you over-evaluate yourself. Pay attention to what you know about it. Experience what your feelings are.

Let an image emerge that represents that experience for you. It can take the form of a person, symbol or pattern. Study it for a while.

When you are ready, open your eyes and draw that image of yourself. When finished, write what this experience evokes in you, how it affects your daily life. Then mark the sheet (2) and turn it over. Let all thoughts and feelings drop away. Relax and be still, close your eyes.

3. You also carry models in you of how *other people* see you.

How they believe you are. The images *they* project on you. These can be positive or negative.

Let us begin with the positive ones of how you are. They have very high expectations of you and you have to live up to those. Check out what they are. Get in touch with how that makes you feel. Let an image come for such experiences. Any symbol or image will do. Communicate with it, get to know it, understand what that means. When you are ready, draw a picture of yourself on half the sheet. Write down what this experience means for you. Put the drawing aside.

Close your eyes and become still. Now bring to mind how people see you in a *negative* way. Imagine their negative projection, what you are that does not live up to their expectations.

Feel what you have internalized from these negative expectations and judgements. Let a picture or image emerge. Communicate with it and understand what it does to you.

When ready, take the previous sheet and on the other half, draw this image. Write down what this experience evokes in you. Mark the sheet (3) and turn it over.

Let go of all the previous models and fall quiet. Close your eyes.

4. Now see the *you* that you *should* be. The glamorous 'secret day-dream' model of how you would like to be, of how you push yourself to *try* to be. This image says that you should be all sorts of incredible, unreal, exaggerated and unattainable things. It prevents you from accepting yourself as you are and keeps you dissatisfied with yourself.

Get a picture and really take a long good look at it, reflect on it and get to know it as much as you can. Stay with it.

When ready, draw what you have experienced and then write about it. Mark the sheet (4).

5. Now pick up all the sheets and arrange them in order. Look at each drawing and get in touch with each model. Name it. Remember your feelings about it. How do you evaluate yourself?

Now stand with your eyes closed. Stay in awareness of all the many feelings and thoughts that these models have stirred up in you.

Allow your body to feel the weight and the limitations of these images and how they ultimately restrict you.

As you stand, let your body move in order to *shake away all the stuff*. You can make sounds as you release the multitudes of images that you carry. Let them slide off, all these false, imposed models that are not you.

6. When ready, sit down and fall still. Feel the freedom of the lifted weight. Find your inner calm. Become centred and calm.

Now get in touch with *your true self*, as you know it to be. Ask yourself, 'What is an image or model that is realistic for me to attain, right now or in the near future? A model of how I could *be*, which is within my potential to become.'

Think *realistically* of what you can become. Get an image from within you of your true potential, the you which *you know to be you*.

Notice what attitudes, qualities, feelings and ideas you have now with this model, see yourself that way. Check what is appropriate and practical and drop anything that does not seem useful. Take some time to do this. When ready, draw and write about this experience.

7. *(Optional)* The last step of this exercise has the purpose of *grounding* this model, of helping to make it a loving and dynamic element in your everyday life. If the model seems good to you, you can then proceed, if not, take time to make any changes or adjustments.

Close your eyes. Visualize yourself as being that model. *Become* that model. Feel what it is like to be it.

See your posture, how does your body feel whilst embodying the qualities?

How do you feel when you view the world out there in this new way? Now visualize yourself, dynamically, in a number of everyday situations in your life, possessing and acting out the qualities and attitudes of the model.

Write down any new insights you would like to remember.

Processing the experience:

Choose a partner to share your drawings and experience with. Spend some time going through your negative self-images, with your partner helping you to come to terms with them and understand how they limit you. Spend a considerable amount of time with your last drawing. What does it really mean to you? What is the major quality or qualities of this drawing? Make sure that none of the negative self-images are creeping into the last drawing. How does this new model fit into your everyday life? What blocks or obstacles in you will need to be explored before you can realistically attain this ideal model? Remember your ideal model represents the next step for you and is not something to use harshly against yourself. Partners should help each other to find a good sense of what this last model involves in a realistic and practical way.

SELF-SHARING: A HOPI INDIAN RITUAL

This is a ritual that the Hopi Indians of North America performed regularly to make a public statement about themselves and about how they felt in their life. Each brought an object which was special and meaningful to share with the group and presented it in a way that evoked a deep sense of wholeness and reverence. It not only symbolized the member's reality but also his place in the larger whole of the community. This ritual provides a positive environment for each participant to be included in the group, builds interpersonal relationships, and explores group dynamics.

Age: seven–adult

Time: Depends upon the number of participants; in a group of twenty, two hours.

Equipment: Each participant is asked either to bring from home an object which symbolizes his life at the moment and what is meaningful and important to him, or to take a walk in nature and find an object which provides the same meaning.

Exercise:

1. Each person take the object that he has brought and quietly form a circle. Sit down and close eyes. Each go to that safe, still place inside you which is special to you. Stay in this place of rest and peace.

Feel the group, sitting here as a whole. Now make silent contact with each one around you. Sense your position here in relation to everyone else.

2. Open your eyes.

Anyone can start the ritual.

Without talking, remaining silent, the first person picks up his object, stands in front of each member, in turn, and silently shows him what it is.

When you have been around to everyone, go to the centre

of the circle and tell the group what the object is and why it has special meaning to you.

Then put the object in the centre of the circle, where you feel it belongs, and returns to your place.

3. Now, one at a time, silently continue in the same way, but as you put your object down, add it to form a sculpture, putting it where you feel it should be.

4. When everyone has participated allow a moment of silence. This sculpture is a symbol of our group, of us together as a community.

Anyone can now go up and make any adjustments or re-arrangements you may wish, to make it more complete, to create a statement of our group.

When everyone is still again, feel the energy of the Group. The Sculpture is a symbol of our *wholeness*.

RESENTMENTS, APPRECIATIONS AND REQUESTS

This simple exercise is good *psychological* toothbrushing, for groups of people that spend a significant amount of time together, a family or a class. There is always a reservoir of unexpressed communications among people who are frequently together—some of them positive, some not. What is unspoken remains *in the air*, implicit yet still influencing the quality of relating. This exercise facilitates honest and clear communication. It demonstrates that it is acceptable to let our feelings and needs be known, but that this doesn't necessarily mean we get what we want every time. It opens the way for participants to learn that they have choices of how to respond to both their own needs and the needs of others.

Age: seven–adult

Time: Can be structured from twenty minutes to one hour, or left open-ended.

Exercise:

The participants sit in a circle. Each individual is free to express whatever feelings, appreciations, resentments or requests they wish, to each other or to the educator. When a participant speaks he looks at the person he is communicating to, starts with that person's name, followed by the communication. For example: 'David, I really appreciate how helpful you were today.' Or, 'Mary, I resent your always taking my best pens.' 'Joan, when you criticize it hurts my feelings.' 'Sam, I would like to play soccer with you.'

The person receiving the communication does not reply or respond. He simply receives it and takes it in. There are no justifications or denials.

LEARNING THROUGH CONFLICTS

Interpersonal conflicts are inevitable for adolescents, who are in the process of finding and establishing their identity, learning to assert their power, and developing their ability to communicate. Often in the *heat of the moment* awareness is lost and understanding of the other person is weak. This exercise provides a means of identifying the conflict, seeing its underlying cause, and exploring alternative behaviours. It develops communication skills and empathic abilities.

Age: twelve–adult

Time: Depending on the situation and incident, thirty minutes to one hour.

Exercise:

Choose a conflict that happened in the classroom.

Designate one group of four to six to be an observer group. Designate one group of four to six to create a still photograph or image of a part of the scene involving the conflict.

The children enacting the conflict form themselves into the image or still photograph symbolizing the conflict. The educator touches each person in this group in turn, and they say what they are feeling about this conflict.

The observing group then asks questions to the players, who answer from the role they are playing. This will show the underlying feelings in the conflict.

The two groups together decide how the situation can be changed or transformed, and eventually the player group must move into another still image to show the transformation. This process can be directed and facilitated by the observer group.

At each stage: A. Identify what the conflict is.

B. Determine the underlying cause of mis-understanding. (Lack of communication, provocation, insecurity, etc.)

C. Discuss what can be done about it.

This exploration produces a fuller picture of what is really happening, as well as potential directions of transformation.

UNDERSTANDING EACH OTHER BETTER

We all have moments of misunderstanding, irritation or anger, with which we would like to learn a better way of coping. What can we do with our negative feelings? It is possible to change our perception of the situation by enlarging our capacity for understanding the other person and jumping into their shoes. This enables us to recognize better both our own feelings and become aware of the feelings of others, which leads to the important social skill of empathy and increases our sensitivity.

Ages: seven to adult

Time: 15 minutes for the exercise

20 minutes for processing the exercise

Equipment: None.

Exercise:

Find a comfortable body position, relax and breathe deeply for a moment or two. We will be doing an empathy exercise and will be jumping into the other person's place in order to understand better a difficult experience we have had.

Now choose an incident or an event in your life recently that felt uncomfortable, irritating or unpleasant, or an incident where there was a misunderstanding between you and another person. Remember a moment like this.

What we will be doing is to relive this incident in our imagination. Don't just think about it, but actually imagine that you are living it again right now. Put yourself back into the environment that you were in during that situation. Where were you? What were you doing? Who was there with you? See it all now as vividly as possible. Look around you. What do you see?

Become aware of how you are feeling in this situation. Now see the other person with whom you had this experience. See how the person is dressed, his or her position in the room, what he or she is doing. Now start living again this incident. The same words, the same feelings, exactly the same interaction. Relive each single word, each single feeling—feel it all now.

As soon as you have relived it entirely, still keeping your eyes closed, you release that memory. Let go of it. Breathe very very deeply and breathe it out of you. Do this several times.

Now you're going to relive again this same incident: except this time you will live it as if you were the other person. Switch places with them. Imagine now that you are the other person and identify with them. You have their feelings, their motivations, their thoughts. What is it like to be that other person? How is your existence? What is life like for you as that other person?

Go through the incident again, step by step, always being that other person. Say again whatever was said and do again whatever was done. Hear what is said to you. Recreate the entire incident from this perspective.

When finished, become yourself again and slowly come back to the room. Be fully back in yourself with your body, your feelings and your mind.

Processing the experience:
Break into small groups to share what this experience was like for you. Were you able to feel what it was like from the other person's place? Can you understand the other better now? What can you learn from this? How do you feel about it all now?*

THE PSYCHOLOGICAL WORKBOOK
Keeping a psychological workbook or diary serves two main functions: it provides a concrete record of the young person's progress and life as a whole; and it works as a valuable form of catharsis and expression. If young people experience anger, confusion, love, joy, and they can put them onto paper, this serves to relieve their mind and feelings. The journal is written for the individual, not for the educator.
Age: twelve–adult
Time: a few minutes regularly each day
Equipment: A notebook of some kind.
Exercise:
The content of the workbook varies according to the

*Adapted from P. Ferrucci, *What We May Be,* (Turnstone Press, 1982).

individual, and can include whatever information is meaningful and relevant. It's best to define the journal as a record of inner unfolding, rather than a diary which records outer events. Written material, drawings and poetry may be included.

The following is a partial list of contents that is useful to record:

1. Responses to exercises done in the class, and a recording of feelings, thoughts or reactions to work done. This helps to deepen experience. It also helps to articulate individual experience more clearly and fully.

2. Responses to meaningful events in life.

3. Imagery: visualizations or experiences in other sensory modalities. This can include images that come spontaneously as well as through structured exercises. They can be recorded in writing and with drawings. It is useful to record feelings and associations in response to the images, and their meaning and interpretation may bring additional insight.

4. Meditation: notes on the results of any meditations used or experimented with, seed ideas or any insights occurring.

5. Peak experiences. A record of times one feels extremely good about oneself. This enables an individual to affirm and recognize his positive self more fully.

6. Negative patterns or hangups that one is aware of in oneself and is working on, vicious circles, fears, worries, and problems that one wants to explore and learn more about. Here it is important for the educator to be available to help and to discuss solutions.

HOW IS IT BETWEEN YOU AND YOUR MIND?

No one would question the importance of the mind and the value of using it skilfully and effectively. The mind can be a healthy servant or an overwhelming tyrant. Not only do our feelings, attitudes, and beliefs influence the way we use our minds, but also our psychological relationship with it has a great impact.

This guided visualization exercise provides a basic assessment of the participant's psychological relationship to his mind and evokes ways to improve the quality of that relationship. As a preparation to this exercise, it is recommended that the body and feelings exercises will have previously been introduced. As a further exploration the FEELING AND MIND INTEGRATION exercise expands awareness, helps to resolve any remaining conflicts, and integrates the two realms.

Age: ten–adult
Time: 30 minutes for the exercise
      30 minutes for processing the experience
Equipment: One sheet of paper and crayons for each participant.
Exercise:

Sit comfortably and relax your body. First let it move or stretch if it needs to, give it a little attention right now.

Now close your eyes and turn your attention towards your inner world. Imagine that you have a jug of water and an empty glass. Imagine that you are pouring water into this glass, filling it to the top without spilling any.

Now multiply twelve by eighteen. In your mind multiply twelve by eighteen and as you do so notice what kind of mental process you go through. What kind of thoughts do you have as you multiply twelve by eighteen?

Now think about an abstract concept, think about growth. What is growth? Think of the variety of things that grow. Think about all the ways you grow. What does growth mean?

Now remember what it is like when you are working on solving a problem. It might be a scientific problem, or a personal problem, or a practical one. What is it like when you're working on a problem and you *can't* find the answer? What happens? Do you feel frustration, irritation, confusion?

Now remember what it's like when you *do* get the answer, when you finally find the answer or solve the problem. What is it like when the light switch has been turned on and you solve it? Everything becomes clear and you know. Everything falls into place. Recall what that experience is like for you.

Now become aware of all these different mental processes we have just been through: filling the glass, multiplying numbers, thinking about growth, struggling with a problem and then solving it. They are all processes of your mind, all different aspects of your mind.

Let an image emerge, an image or a symbol that

represents your mind. It will be an image for how you experience your mind. It might not make *sense*, but accept whatever image comes. Allow it to become vivid and clear.

As the image emerges, take a good, long look at it. What is your initial feeling reaction to this image? What is its quality and energy? How does it make you feel?

This image has something to communicate to you about your mind. It may be with or without words, listen to its message. It may want to talk to you. Let it tell you how it feels towards you. How do you feel towards your mind? Enter into a dialogue with the image for your mind. Find out what it wants from you, or needs from you. Tell it what you want and need from it.

Now for a moment, step into this image for your mind and become it. You can put it on as if it were a shirt or a dress. What is it like to *be* this image? What is your existence? What is your life like as this image? What do you have to offer?

Now become yourself again and continue the dialogue. See if you can establish better relations with each other. Make friends. You might want to reach some agreements as to what you will do for each other in the future. When you feel ready, say goodbye to the image for your mind and come back to the room.

Take some time now to draw your *sense* or experience of this image. After drawing, write about this experience. Write down the way you feel about it and how you experience your mind.

Processing the experience:
Break into groups of three or four to share your experience. Focus your discussion on the needs of your mind as well as what it has to offer you. If there was any conflict between your feelings and your mind, how might they be resolved? Group members should help each other explore their experiences.

FEELING AND MIND INTEGRATION ON THE MOUNTAIN

This visualization is recommended for all adolescents. A foreground issue for them is the relationship between their feelings and their mind. Allowing the mind to respect and include the feelings is paramount. Major conflicts can occur, and the adolescent needs to realize that *both* domains are important and useful.

The visualization can be started with the participants looking at the drawings for their feelings and mind if previously done, or by guiding them to create an image symbolic of each.

Age: twelve–adult

Time: 20 minutes for the exercise

30 minutes for processing the experience

Exercise:

Spend a few minutes looking at your drawing of your feelings and of your mind. What impression do you get from them? Are they in conflict, or do they seem to go together well? How do you feel about each of them? Are you drawn towards one or the other? Does one have more energy for you than the other? Would you like either of them to be different? How?

Now close your eyes, spend a few minutes relaxing. Breathe deeply. Now imagine that you are in a meadow. It is a beautiful spring day and the sun is shining. With you in the meadow are your images for your feelings and your mind. The three of you are there together and you are all experiencing the beauty of the day, and the fresh clean air. Take a moment to be in the meadow now. What is the meadow like? What are you wearing? Just explore your environment for a few moments.

Spend a few minutes watching the images for your feelings and your mind as you all walk through the meadow together. See how they go along together. Notice how they relate to each other. What are they saying to each other? To you? You have no sense of rush and there is nothing you *have* to do.

If you'll look in the distance you see a very tall mountain at the end of the meadow. As you look at the mountain you know that you are going to climb that mountain with your images. The three of you are going to climb together. So begin walking together towards the mountain.

Begin climbing the mountain now, taking your images for your feelings and mind with you. As you climb you can feel your body climbing, the muscles in your legs and the earth beneath your feet. You feel strong and supple and your images are there with you. As you climb you can take time to interact with your feelings and your mind.

Together you continue getting higher and higher. You even begin to have a sense of height now and the air is very clear and there is a cool breeze. If feelings and mind are not with you now, they come and join you, as you climb higher and higher.

You climb to a place that has a beautiful stream running through it and you can stop and refresh yourself by drinking some of the cool water. Then you turn around and look behind you at the great distance you have come and you feel satisfaction with your ability to climb.

You are very near to the top now, the three of you together. As you reach the top the three of you stop and stand in a circle on top of the mountain and feel the sun shine down. You all feel very good that you have made this great climb. Stand for a few moments and allow the warm sunlight to shine on you. The sunshine envelops all of you in its warmth. The images may change slightly at this point. If they do, just let it happen.

You may also want to have a conversation with your feelings and mind here. See if they have anything more to say to you or you to them. Notice also how they are relating to each other now on top of the mountain, in the sunshine.

When you feel ready you can come back down the mountain and bring yourself here to this room. Take a few moments to come back, gradually beginning to hear again the sounds in the room and from outside if there are any. Come back at your own speed or pace. When you're back take a few moments to write in your journal about this experience. Pay special attention to any insights you might have had with feelings and mind and any ways you discovered that they might get along better and more harmoniously.

Processing the experience:
Break into groups of three or four to share this experience. What did you learn about your feelings and your mind? How can you apply what you learned to your everyday life? How can your feelings and your mind get along better? Group members should help each other in any way appropriate.

PREPARATORY STAGE TO MEDITATION
The following is a brief preparation to using meditation of any

kind and is also useful before guided imagery work. To relax and focus the mind, and to enable the participant to be fully present with their experience, can increase the results of the work.

1. *Physical relaxation:* requires putting the body in a comfortable position and reducing, as far as possible, any bodily tensions.

2. *Emotional composure:* a quieting of the feelings and their activity to approach a state of calm, relaxed serenity.

3. *Mental recollection:* the direction of the mind's interest and attention inwards.

WHAT WE MAY BE: THE EVOCATION OF AN IDEAL QUALITY
(1) REFLECTIVE AND RECEPTIVE MEDITATION

The purpose of this meditative work is to evoke a realistic and attainable quality, and to establish a more balanced way of being in the world. It also provides a basic model of meditation which can be applied to any chosen topic. It is an effective way of reinforcing a positive quality that is trying to emerge, and of evoking a quality that one needs to develop.

Meditation follows the principle that energy follows thought, and meditating on these qualities will tend to evoke them. At times it may also energize the obstacles or blocks to that quality in the meditator. This is a natural occurrence and need not cause concern. Such obstacles may be viewed as *opportunities for growth* and attention can be given to resolve the obstacle in case it arises.

It is advisable to choose a quality or topic for meditation which has particular meaning to the meditator, and one that he is sincerely interested in developing. Following the exercise is a list of Transpersonal Qualities. The list is not exhaustive and other possibilities may be chosen to focus on with this form of meditation.

Age: fourteen–adult
Time: 20 to 30 minutes for the meditation
      20 minutes for processing the experience
Equipment: Writing materials.
Exercise:
Choose a quality that you would like to develop in yourself, or that you already experience within yourself but would like

more of. Each person shares his quality with the rest of the group.

Now take some time to write about this quality. Write *all* that you are aware of about this quality. This stage is called reflection or pondering. To ponder on this quality means to focus one's thoughts carefully so as to understand it better. What does this quality mean to you? What are all the different aspects of it? (10 minutes.)

Now we have just spent time discovering what we already know or have experienced about this quality. Sit comfortably, close your eyes and breathe deeply a few times. Imagine that you are taking all of these thoughts and ideas you have just had and are placing them on top of your head. Gather them all there. Let them float to the top of your head and allow your mind to clear as you do so.

Allow yourself to be open and receptive. Be silent and still. Now imagine that a ray of sunlight shines on all these words and thoughts on top of your head. Allow yourself to be receptive to the energy of the sun. Let all the words and thoughts be energized by the light and see what happens.

Now that you have cleared your mind, you have space for new insights and awareness to come. Imagine something new to be coming in with this ray of sunlight. Be open and don't censor. Allow whatever insights or images to come that want to come. At any point you may want to stop and make notes on your experience. Any time you want you can close your eyes and be receptive again. Find a rhythm that's right for you between writing and being receptive. I'll give you about ten minutes to do this stage at your own pace.

Optional stage:
To complete this meditation, let's all stand up. Take a moment to feel this quality you have been meditating on inside you, in your body. Start moving and walking around the room with that quality alive and being expressed through your body and walking. How would you be with it inside you and being expressed through your walk? Exaggerate whatever you are doing right now in order to experience it more fully.

Now introduce yourself to others here as this quality, affirming its potential within you. For example: I'm Mary and I am self-confident. Take a little time to meet a few people here and other qualities here.

Processing the experience:
Find a partner and share your meditation with them.

TRANSPERSONAL QUALITIES
Beauty
Compassion
Comprehension
Courage
Creativity
Energy Power
Enthusiasm
Eternity Infinity Universality
Freedom Liberation Detachment
Co-operation Friendship Brotherhood
Generosity
Goodness
Goodwill
Gratitude Appreciation Admiration Wonder
Harmony
Humour
Inclusiveness
Joy Bliss
Light
Love
Order
Patience
Positiveness
Reality Truth
Renewal
Trust Faith
Serenity Peace
Service
Silence Quiet Calm
Simplicity
Synthesis Wholeness
Understanding
Vitality
Will
Wisdom

MEDITATING ON THINGS THAT INTEREST ME

This variation of *reflective* and *receptive* meditation is called a seed thought. The focus for meditation here can be on a *seed thought*, a particular idea, or on a physical object. It can facilitate and support classroom study, for example, in a biology class to meditate on an object of nature (rock, bark, pine cones, feathers, flowers, etc.). Alternatively it can be used to explore a theoretical concept like the structure of poetry.

Age: twelve–adult

Time: 20 minutes for the exercise

20 minutes for processing the experience

Equipment: One large sheet of paper and coloured pens for each participant

Exercise:

In the centre of the page, write the topic for meditation. It can be a seed thought, word or phrase or object of any kind. Each individual may choose his own topic or the entire class may focus on the same one.

Begin to reflect or think about your chosen topic for meditation. Begin to explore your subject. What do you know about it? As you think of something you know about it, draw a line out from the centre and write it onto the line, like a spoke to a wheel. (See example; educator demonstrate on the board.) (10 minutes.)

If you find yourself drifting away from your subject, gently bring yourself back to it. Don't get angry or irritated with yourself, we all tend to drift away. (For example, a tree. A tree is life. It protects. A tree is solid and gives nourishment to the environment . . . it really was hot yesterday . . . I hope it's not tomorrow . . . I remember last summer . . . oh goodness, look where I am . . . I'll never be able to meditate.) When you find this drifting happening, just return to your topic of meditation. If we force our mind it will not co-operate.

Explore these major areas of your topic: forms; qualities; purpose; functions. Spend fifteen minutes with this section.

Processing the experience:

Break into partners or small groups and share the results of your meditation.

MEDITATING IN GROUPS

Meditation can initially be made more enjoyable and energetic by group participation. The topic for focus is then the same for all participants. Any of the forms of meditation can be used: an ideal or transpersonal quality, a seed thought or an object. Meditating in groups still serves the same purposes as individual meditation, mental development, etc. but adds an interpersonal element.

To meditate in groups, divide participants into groups of four to six people. They are guided in the same way as individual meditations, with short breaks for sharing between the various stages. Appropriate time would be ten minutes for a stage of meditation and ten minutes for sharing that stage and so on.

CONFRONTING SOCIAL ISSUES

Young people today are often concerned about current social issues which directly or indirectly affect the quality of their life and their vision of the future. If unaddressed these issues (like unemployment, social discrimination, the threat of nuclear war, human rights and so on) can silently fester and disturb their sense of well-being; or they can be a source of anger and rebellion towards the adult world. Confronting a social issue which troubles young people can provide a forum for: the release of negative feelings and feelings of impotence; an exploration of the causes and factors that created the issue; a collective discovery of what could be done about it; and the opportunity for some personal action and the liberation that inevitably comes with the acknowledgement of the problem.

The following exercise provides a format which can be used to address *any* social issue. I recommend that the issue to be explored is chosen by the students, rather than the educator.

Age: fourteen-adult

Time: Minimum 1½ hours, length to be determined by educator.

Equipment: Writing materials.

Exercise:

Form small groups of 4 to 6 people.

1. Take a few minutes, each of you, to reflect on and write about the social issue which your group will be exploring. First write down how you *feel* about this issue. What kind of

thoughts do you have about it? What opinions and beliefs does it stir up in you regarding the nature of people and the world? (Do this for 10–15 minutes.)

Share what you have written with your group. Make sure each group member has the opportunity to speak. (Allow enough time for each participant to have at least 5 minutes to speak.)

2. Close your eyes and take a few quiet breaths. You have heard many feelings, many opinions and ideas about this issue. Allow all of that input to be in your consciousness.

Now close your eyes and allow an image which symbolizes this social issue to emerge. Don't censor or judge your image—just let it come into your mind's eye. Allow the symbol to become vivid and clear.

Take a good look at it. How do you feel as you see it? What does it communicate to you? What thoughts does it evoke?

Now open your eyes and take a moment to write about the image.

Close your eyes again and let go of the previous image. Breathe it away. Let's take a leap for a moment and imagine that this issue has a creative resolution: although you may have absolutely no idea of what it is. Now allow another image to emerge, which symbolizes the creative resolution of this issue—of what needs to happen with this issue. Be receptive and wait for this image to come. It will most likely be quite vague and symbolic. Don't censor or push anything away.

Allow the symbol to become vivid and clear. It may not make sense to you yet and this is okay. When you have the image, look at it for a moment. What is its quality? Its meaning? If it could communicate with you, what could be its message? Take as much time as you need. When you're ready, come back and draw the image and write about it.

3. With your group, share your two images and their meaning. Begin to search together for a creative possibility of how this issue might ultimately be resolved—both on a large scale and in terms of what *you* as a group might do about it. Don't limit your discussion—think the absurd, let your minds be creative, don't worry about details yet. You may find a common idea being expressed by several people or a common quality needed to resolve this issue, like more love in the

world, or more appreciation of differences. (This discussion could last any length of time.)

4. As a group, focus your discussion onto what you as *individuals* might choose to do about this issue. If you were free and willing, what appropriate actions could/would you choose to take? Be concrete and specific. For example, write to your local M.P., form a work group, organize a public lecture, hold a rally, ask your parents to do something, raise money for a voluntary group with some sponsored activity, give an evening a week to a voluntary group, etc. Remember that your possibilities need to be harmless to yourself and to others and to the environment. Your possible actions can cover a wide range from physical tasks to choosing to live your life with more of a certain quality, like love, or a certain attitude, like positive regard.

Brainstorm as many concrete possibilities as you can. Don't limit yourselves. (This discussion again could vary in time.)

5. Elect a spokesman for your group. Choose the best six of your suggestions for the resolution of this issue. Bring them back to the larger group. Each small-group spokesperson share the six suggestions.

(*Note:* If a class project is made of the social issue, the work could go further into the implementation of these actions.)

Chapter 4

EACH OF US IS A CROWD

Eleven-year-old Mary rises early in order to have time with her mother before her mother goes to work and Mary to school. This special time for both Mary and her mother is spent quietly reading a book and talking about the coming day. Mary cherishes this moment when her mother is very loving to her and she tends to regress to behaviour which is younger than her age would suggest. She actively seeks security and her mother's affection and behaves in a clearly childish way, evoking from her mother feelings of protectiveness and of wanting to hold and cuddle Mary.

Mary leaves for school, meets her friend, and already Mary appears to be quite a different person. With her friend, Mary is more grown up, boasting about her good marks in art, and appearing in general to be self-confident and at ease. She tells her friend what they should do after school and decides what games they will play at break-time. Clearly she is the leader in this relationship, with her friend taking a subservient role.

On the way to school Mary and her friend meet two boys from class, and again Mary's behaviour changes. Now she is aggressive and boisterous, teasing the boys and provoking their irritation, even to the point of pushing one of them out of her way. She clearly does not like one of the boys and tells him so both verbally and through her behaviour.

Upon arrival at school, when the maths class begins, Mary's behaviour again changes quite dramatically; now she seems confused, near to tears, and unable to work. She seeks constant assistance from the teacher, does not understand the task at hand, and is caught cheating by copying another child's work. When confronted with this behaviour, she bursts into tears—saying that she is stupid and unable to do maths and a failure.

That afternoon in art class, her favourite activity, Mary excels brilliantly, showing great artistic talent and creativity. She is bright, co-operative and contributing to the aliveness in the room. She helps other children, demonstrating sensitivity and compassion.

In a short period of time Mary has demonstrated five different and disparate behaviours. She *appears* to be many different people and may feel confused by her own inconsistent behaviour, sometimes thinking that there must be something *wrong* with her. She may be frightened by her aggressive behaviour and try to counteract it by being a very good girl. There are so many different parts of us, and such a variety of behaviours and internal states into which we fall, that it all seems beyond our conscious control. Sometimes we may feel that we are several different people, in spite of ourselves. When a child misbehaves, he often feels that he did it in spite of himself—that he did not really want to be difficult or to cause the trouble for which he is reprimanded.

Just as a child may find that he behaves differently in different situations, so too do adults—even educators. Obviously, our behaviour as an educator varies according to what is happening in our own life, how we are feeling, and how our children are behaving. Our internal state can swing quite suddenly from patience and compassion to irritation and disgust. Our headmaster walks into the room, and we become the *ideal* teacher, skilfully directing the class; we may be acutely aware of our need to impress him with our educational talents. When Mary is confused and crying during maths, we may sometimes feel compassion towards her and patiently help her through her difficult moment. Whereas at another moment, perhaps because it's been a hectic morning, we find that we are sick and tired of this behaviour and pay her no attention, feeling it's time she learned not to be such a baby.

We can easily perceive our own multiplicity by noticing how often we modify our outlook on life, our self-image, our perception of others, our behaviour towards others and our experience of our self internally. Life may appear to us to be: a struggle, a wonderful dance, a burdensome chore, a nightmare, an opportunity, a joyful play, a fulfilling task or a meaningless existence. One way of perceiving this multiplicity is through the model of *subpersonalities*.

Subpersonalities are autonomous configurations within the personality as a whole. They are psychological identities, co-existing as a multitude of lives within one person; each subpersonality has specific behaviour patterns and individual characteristics forming a relatively unified whole. Each has a *style* and motivation of its own which is often surprisingly dissimilar from that of other subpersonalities. In a sense, each of us is a crowd. In a child there can be the co-operative learner, the brilliant artist, the super reader, the rebel, the regressed baby, the organizer, the teacher's pet, the class clown, the loving friend, the boy-hater, the sneaky saboteur, the adorable doll, the mature leader, the fearful exam-taker, the pretending adapter, and so on. In the educator, there may be the frustrated mother, the bored babysitter, the fulfilled saint, the sacrificing martyr, the failed actress, the analytical psychologist, the intolerant authority, the irritated idealist, the tired giver, the patient facilitator, the rigid pragmatist, or the knowledgeable professor. Each one of these disparate characters or subpersonalities will demonstrate postures and even unique physical states; it will have its own emotional quality, and will possess a mental outlook with accompanying beliefs, attitudes and world-view.

Each subpersonality has its own way of relating and responding. Very often they are *reactive* to the environment and are stimulated by events. For example, if I return from work and find the house in a mess, my 'women's libber' subpersonality springs up, I feel angry and refuse to cook dinner. If a child misbehaves, the educator may find his 'intolerant authority' subpersonality appears; whereas if that same child is frightened, the 'patient facilitator' may emerge. Likewise a child may behave in co-operative and sensitive ways in the classroom, but transform into a monster at home.

A great limitation to a child's development, and to the emergence of his own unique personality, may occur when he identifies strongly with a parent, and that identification is so complete that he becomes a living portrait of that parent, possessing all the parent's mannerisms and idiosyncrasies. The subpersonality model can be used to relieve this unhealthy state by shifting attention to other subpersonalities, even to unknown ones, to enable him to break away from his identification.

If an individual is identified with any one subpersonality, he experiences that he *is* that subpersonality and consequently loses access to the rest of his personality. For example, if I am identified with a predominantly emotional subpersonality, I am governed by my feelings and am cut off from my rational mind. Or if I am identified with a professorial subpersonality, I may be cut off from my feelings or even my intuition. Subpersonalities themselves are not limiting; our unconscious identification with them can be.

Assagioli described the incongruity that sometimes arises between subpersonalities when he wrote:

> We are not unified; we often feel that we are, because we do not have many bodies or many limbs, and because one hand doesn't usually hit the other. But, metaphorically, that is exactly what does happen within us. Several subpersonalities are continually scuffling: impulses, desires, principles, aspirations are engaged in an unceasing struggle.[1]

Ideally we want accessibility to our entire personality in order to choose appropriate behaviour according to our life situation. Our subpersonalities are like players in an orchestra; with each instrument playing its own music, disharmony and perhaps chaos will result. Obviously the orchestra needs a conductor who will direct the instruments through a harmonious symphony. *All* the players are needed, though at times one or another may be called upon to perform individually. Very often our day-to-day experience is that of disharmony in the orchestra, with the different parts of us seeking expression and unconsciously controlling our behaviour, rather than being organized in a complementary way.

For educators there are three primary uses of the subpersonality model: for skill development, remedially and for self-knowledge.

Skill Development

On an abstract level we may know that each child has an inner
knowing or capacity to learn, but it is important for a child
himself to realize that he has these creative resources within
him. One of the best ways to facilitate this awareness is to
show him that he has *already* done something well; for
example, to remind him of an occasion when he was reading
well and that his 'super reader' subpersonality exists. If he then
adopts this subpersonality, he is likely to enjoy it and succeed.
Alternatively, an educator can encourage a child to imagine
that he has a capable subpersonality coming into being and
this will produce a similar effect. The *creating* of a subpersonality provides a concrete, vivid *ideal model* of the
successful learning of any subject or skill, which then has a
tendency to become real. Such modelling is a playful and
effective tool for drawing out latent skills as well as for
reinforcing existing ability. It also has the effect of aiding the
creation of the positive self-image, so vital for a child.

Remedial Use of Subpersonalities

It is also important that the child or adolescent becomes aware
of the destructive, less developed or negative parts in himself,
which often obstruct his life and his learning. It can be a relief
for a child to recognize that he has many different parts, some
of which he is glad to have and others which cause him
difficulty. Children are often perplexed by the variations in
their behaviour, and recognition helps them to understand
themselves. Awareness liberates children to behave differently
and helps them to come to terms with their negative
behaviour. Familiarity with subpersonalities creates a healthy
psychological distance between the child and the forces that
may take him over. To objectify and make a subpersonality
visible, coloured, and concrete, gives the child the opportunity
to know and to *master* it.

One effective way to work with subpersonalities is to
invite a group of children to make a mask of the part of them
which they hide from the rest of the class. Invariably, angry
demons, crying clowns and frightened fairies appear among
the masks. For many, this process of creating the mask turns
something dark and threatening into something playful and
light; it brings the difficulty out into the *open* and provides an

opportunity to redeem and transform it.

Self-knowledge
By deepening our acquaintance with our subpersonalities we are able to know ourselves more fully. To have a clear awareness of our subpersonalities is to know our strengths, weaknesses, gifts and limitations. To recognize the multiplicity of our personality is to build a realistic perception of the whole, rather than living as if we were merely this or that part, this or that behaviour. The increased self-knowledge gleaned from subpersonality awareness will also reveal resources, latent qualities and hidden potentials. For adolescents, it is a good preparation for uncovering the 'I' or permanent centre, in contradistinction to the transitory nature of subpersonalities.

How To Work With Subpersonalities
Many subpersonalities are psychologically healthy and do not require further attention beyond their recognition and appropriate use. Such parts as the 'super reader' or the 'creative clown' are surely positive contributions to a child's life. Getting to know a subpersonality, how and when it manifests, and what it has to contribute is essential and leads to the ability to choose behaviour consciously.

An effective and playful way to work with a subpersonality is to give it a name: to name is to know. To give a subpersonality a name that has meaning is to embody it with more life and definition, which consequently makes it more accessible. For example, when I am behaving as my 'Doris Day' subpersonality and being overly positive, I know that my insecurity has control of me and it's time for me to take charge again. Naming a subpersonality can be like making a new friend. We eventually get to know that person and learn to love them *in spite of* and *with* their flaws. Children and adolescents often enjoy playing the game of naming their subpersonalities and presenting them to others. Some examples given by children, which illustrate the breadth and variety of subpersonalities, are Silly Sally, Joe Cool, Caring Carol, Doubting Thomas, Betty Bright, Sensitive Sam, Sexy Sara, Merry Mary, Dennis the Menace, Grumpy Grover, Red Robert, Generous George and Billy Liar.

Although on the surface some subpersonalities appear

negative and distorted, it is important that they be *accepted*. Rather than attempting to get rid of, repress or control subpersonalities, the aim is to transform them and ultimately use them in a positive way. If the educator conveys the feeling that some of them are bad and should be denied or negated, the child will do just that. Giving a subpersonality the right to exist means acknowledging that every part of the personality has something to contribute. By accepting and including a subpersonality it is given the psychological space to grow. The instrument may need tuning, may need to learn how to play in harmony with the other instruments, or may even need to learn how to make music at all, but it cannot do so if it is thrown out of the orchestra. In fact, if we attempt to throw it away, it is likely to increase its negative manifestations and trouble us more.

We all have basic human needs such as the need for love and security, for self-assertion and affirmation, for approval and recognition, which in themselves are not problematic. To transform a subpersonality into a positive contributor, it is necessary to look *behind* its superficial behaviour. It will have an unfulfilled need of some kind and the surface, seemingly negative, behaviour is usually a crude attempt or a learned way of fulfilling the need. The external behaviour of a difficult subpersonality may be harsh and demanding and may create a negative effect on the environment. If a child is displaying difficult behaviours, like tantrums or rebellious assertions, we can ask ourselves what need is behind this behaviour. By accepting the behaviour as a communication, however strong and distorted, and by hearing its message, we can find its need. Furthermore, by responding to the need, the negative behaviour is often alleviated. This kind of *listening* is a form of perception to be cultivated.

If the child or adolescent knows his predominant subpersonalities, he can often determine the unfulfilled need. At least he can co-operate with his educator in finding the need and in exploring more appropriate, acceptable and fulfilling ways to meet it. The child and the educator then become allies rather than adversaries. As the child's awareness develops, he can begin to examine the options and choices available and can experiment with new ways of being.

Subpersonalities are like people. If we treat them with

compassion and understanding they open up and give us the best of what they truly are. The possibility for transformation always exists—*if* we are willing to accept and explore the deeper levels of a subpersonality.

Even each seemingly negative subpersonality ultimately has something to offer, usually in the form of a transpersonal quality. The next step is to find ways in which this quality can be expressed. All subpersonalities carry a *hidden potential*. A frightened child subpersonality may have compassion and sensitivity to express. An aggressive bully may inherently know how to be strong and autonomous. The clown may know how to make people happy. The searching philosopher knows that there can be rich meaning in life. The critic subpersonality often contains within it the ability to discriminate.

Time and time again in subpersonality work with children and adolescents I have been awed by its transformative capacity. I have seen demonic angry witches become strong sensitive young women, arrogant bullies turn into loving protectors, and weeping wimps become understanding supporters. Just as what we repress tends to remain in its unhealthy form, what we accept and creatively work with tends to blossom.

EXERCISES

WHAT PART OF YOU FEELS THAT WAY?
Children often have recurring problems or difficulties with behaviour. With all the good will possible it is not always readily clear, to the child, *how* to deal with the problem and why he behaves in a certain way. This subpersonality exercise helps to bring to the surface that part of him it is that creates the problem behaviour and shows what can be done to correct it. It enables the child to objectify and gain distance from its control over him, and helps him to experience that the problem is not *all* of him.
Age: eight–adult
Time: 30 minutes for the exercise
        30 minutes for processing the experience
Exercise: Drawing materials, crayons and paper *or* Plasticine or clay.

Exercise:

Get in touch with a recurring difficulty you are having. Perhaps it is with other people, or your parents or teacher— some difficulty that you would like to change and be different. Remember what this difficulty is like, how it feels, how you behave with it, what effect it has upon those around you, what you say and do when you are experiencing it. Let all the feelings come up that go with this difficulty.

Where are you when you usually have this difficulty? Who are you usually with? Is there something going on that tends to trigger it? How do you feel about it all?

Now sit comfortably, close your eyes and take a few deep breaths. There is some part of you that creates this problem. It is not all of you. Slowly now, begin to let this feeling take the shape of a person in your imagination. It will be a person who symbolizes this feeling of difficulty and who *is* the problem. If this difficulty were a person, what kind of person would it be? Allow an image to appear for this part of you involved in the problem. It can be any kind of person that you see. What does this person look like? How is he or she dressed? What is the expression on its face?

As you look at this person, how do you feel? What is your reaction? If you could talk to this person what would you say? Begin to talk to this image now and say whatever you feel like saying. Tell it how you feel towards it and about the difficulty it creates in your life.

Now imagine that you, for a moment, become this person. Put it on as if it were a shirt or a dress. What does it feel like to *be* this character? What is life like for you? What is your existence? What is it that you really need? What is it deep inside you that you want? See if you can get in touch with that . . . What are you trying to get most of the time?

Now become yourself again, and continue to have a conversation with this person. See if there is anything you want to say to it about what it needs. Find a way to get along better and to establish a better relationship. Can you make friends somehow? Is there any way you can give this part what it needs?

When you are ready, come back to this room and either draw or sculpt this part of you that has this difficulty and problem.

Processing the experience:
In small groups, or with the entire group, each person can present his drawing or sculpture and what it means to him and what he discovered. Share what this part needs most deeply and explore how you might find other ways of meeting that need.

SUBPERSONALITY MASKS

This exercise takes the form of *creative play*, which gives participants the opportunity to explore subpersonalities that might otherwise be too threatening to bring out. By making a mask of a subpersonality, we objectify it and make more explicit our awareness of it. The mask can be put on and taken off at will, providing the experience of both being it and having the power not to be it, as well as being *more* than it. This can help the participant to *own* both very negative and positive subpersonalities which were previously suppressed. The masks create an active and energetic forum for the experience and the understanding of a subpersonality.
Age: seven–adult
Time: one and a half hours
Equipment: Coloured paper, yarn, sticky labels, stars and shapes, scissors, glue, coloured tissue paper, scotch tape, white paper, string, and any artistic materials appropriate for mask making.
Exercise:
In the centre of the room are many different kinds of material for making a mask. We are each going to make a mask of a particular part of us. We will have about forty-five minutes to make the mask. Take your time and be creative. You can use the materials in whatever way you wish.

Let's first get in touch with the part of us we will make the mask of. Close your eyes, spend a moment to quiet down inside and relax. The mask you will make today will be of the part of you that you hide from the world; that part of you that you don't usually let anyone know is there, and perhaps even you sometimes try very hard to keep it hidden. It can be absolutely any kind of part of you. Think for a moment about what part of you you do not like other people to know you have. As you do this, imagine a mask that shows this. When you are ready open your eyes and begin to work.

(Optional aspects for masks: a feeling you keep secret from others; the part of you you present to the world; for strength building—a part of you that you like and feel good about; for skill building—the part of you that knows how to read, do maths, science, etc.)

Upon completion of the masks, let's all put our mask on and walk around the room and introduce ourselves to each other. Say who you are and what you are like as this mask.

Now find a partner to be with and sit down with your mask beside you. Each take a turn to share your mask with your partner and talk about what the person in the mask needs in order to be understood better and accepted. What does he or she really need? Also find out from the mask what it might eventually like to do, how it would really like to be.

KNOW YOURSELF BETTER

Subpersonality work is an excellent means of acquiring increased self-knowledge and expanding awareness. It can provide a practical method for discovering both areas of strength and psychological aspects that are seeking attention. By allowing elements within us to take human-like shape and form we can both get to know and understand ourselves better. This guided visualization has the purpose of bringing to light those subpersonalities which are most presently active and which require inclusion. It also provides a means of learning what unfulfilled need, if any, is present, as well as enabling the participant to explore what potential contribution it may make.

Age: ten–adult
Time: 20 minutes for the exercise
20 minutes for processing the experience
Exercise:
Sit comfortably, relax and find a quiet place inside. Imagine that you are in a meadow on a beautiful spring day. The sun is shining and the sky is blue. It's a lovely day and you are surrounded by green nature. Take some time now to be in your meadow. Feel yourself there walking through the meadow. Perhaps you can feel the ground beneath your feet, a cool breeze on your face as well as the warmth of the sun.

Across the meadow, at the end of it, there is a cottage. It is quite far away but you can see it. Look at the cottage. What does it look like? You begin to walk towards the cottage and as you do so you are interested to see who or what lives in it.

As you get closer you begin to sense that in this cottage live your subpersonalities. Perhaps you can even hear voices inside. Now you are quite close.

The cottage door opens and two or three of your subpersonalities come out. They are talking intently. You just watch for a moment and notice *who* comes out of the cottage, what they look like and how they are dressed. As they come near you, one of the subpersonalities comes over to you and begins talking to you. Have a dialogue with it. What do you want to say to it? Tell your subpersonality how you feel towards it. See how it feels towards you. What is its reaction to you? Find out what it wants from you. Tell it what you want from it.

Now imagine that you *become* this subpersonality. Identify with it. You can put it on as if it were a shirt or a dress. What is it like to *be* this subpersonality? As this subpersonality, what do you essentially need? What do you *really* need?

Now become yourself again and continue your conversation with this subpersonality. You may be communicating with each other with or without words. See if you can get to know each other better and establish a better relationship with each other. How can you get along better? Can you find out what this subpersonality has to offer or contribute? Ask it. I'll give you a few minutes now to finish up this communication.

Your subpersonality now leaves you and walks back into the meadow and joins the other subpersonalities. The three of them go back inside the cottage. You are left there in the meadow, feeling the warmth of the sun, enjoying the day. When you feel ready, bring yourself back to this room and take a few minutes to write down what happened during this experience for you.

Processing the experience:
Find a partner to share this experience with. Share what subpersonalities you saw and which one came to meet you. What was the nature of your relationship with that subpersonality? Did you already know this part of you? When in your everyday life is it around? What did it need? Is there any way that you can give it what it needs? Were you able to discover

what this subpersonality had to offer? What does this experience tell you about your everyday life?

THE DANCE OF THE SELVES

In this exercise, a recurrent feeling or difficulty is given its right proportions through evoking its opposite and through providing the experience of choice and inner freedom. If we experience a part of ourselves, more deeply and with the body, we can both understand and take charge of it. By taking charge and directing, we experience that who we are is more than the recurrent feeling or difficulty and hence we are empowered to change.

Age: fourteen to adult

Time: 20 minutes for the exercise

      15 minutes for processing the experience

Exercise:

Before starting, choose a recurrent feeling you have that troubles you. It can be any feeling, for example, fear, insecurity or anger. If you know a subpersonality that has this feeling you can choose that subpersonality.

Now stand, spread around the room, so that you have a little space to move. Stand with your legs about shoulder width apart and with your arms hanging loosely at your sides. Close your eyes and take a few deep breaths. Begin to focus your attention and awareness on this feeling or subpersonality you have chosen. Let it begin to come alive inside you. It may not be too comfortable, and that is okay. Remember the feelings this produces, and perhaps you know some thoughts that go with it.

Now begin to allow your body to take on a physical posture that reflects this feeling or subpersonality. It is as if you can become a symbolic statue of this. Really let your body express this part of you now.

When you feel ready, begin to move around and express this part of you through your body. Let your movements and sounds express it. Dance this subpersonality or feeling right now. Be creative and move as you feel drawn to. Even exaggerate what you are dancing right now. See if there is a sound that comes with this movement. (Educator: allow this movement to continue for as long as appropriate.)

Now stop moving and come to a quiet place inside

yourself. Take a few more deep breaths. Imagine now that you also have living inside you the exact opposite of what you have just been. What would the polar opposite of this be for you? It could be anything. For example, if your feeling was fear, what is the opposite of fear for you? Take a moment to discover what the opposite of it would be.

Now begin to allow yourself to feel the opposite feelings and think the opposite thoughts. What would they be like? Really let this opposite experience begin to grow right now. As you do that, allow your body to begin to express and dance this opposite as you did before. Let your body take the physical posture of the opposite, let it move freely, expressing this. See if there is a sound that comes with it. (Again allow appropriate time.)

Now stop moving and again come to a quiet place inside yourself. Stand comfortably, arms held loosely at your sides. Imagine that on one side of you is the first feeling or subpersonality that you were working with and on the other side of you is its opposite. Take a moment to imagine clearly each of these beside you, with you standing in the middle of the two.

When you feel ready, *choose* to step into the first part and experience that physically again and by your own choice, then *choose* to move to the opposite. I'll give you some time now to make a symbolic dance between these two opposites, with you *choosing* and *directing* when and how you move. Do this very slowly in order to experience the transition you make as you direct yourself to move and how it feels for you to *choose* to move between these two poles. Make this symbolic dance back and forth at least three times.

When you are finished, just come back to the place in the middle and again experience yourself with each feeling or subpersonality on one side of you. Be silent for a few moments to absorb your experience.

Processing the experience:
Find a partner to share with. What was your experience like for you? What did you learn about yourself from it? *How* was it that you were able to move and direct yourself between two very different polarities? What does this mean? Is it possible that you have more power to choose than you realize?

TRANSFORMATION

With the use of guided imagery it is possible to create the symbolic psychological situation for a subpersonality to be transformed into its latent potential. This symbolic process tends to stimulate the unconscious to follow suit. To be aware of a potential transformation provides inspiration to allow this unfoldment to happen in reality. This exercise provides the opportunity for a subpersonality to reveal its true nature, and provides the participant with an ideal model of what lies within the subpersonality, as well as some practical steps to take.

Age: fourteen–adult
Time: 20 minutes for the exercise
       20 minutes for processing the experience
Equipment: Psychological workbook.
Exercise:

Sit in a comfortable body position, relax for a few moments and find a quiet place inside. Choose a subpersonality that you know quite well and perhaps have worked with before. Let it take some shape and form. What kind of person is it? Is it a man or a woman? Old or young? See it clearly before you and let it be with you right now. Let a vivid and clear image come for this part of you. Realize that it is a totality, with its own way of being in the world, its own style and mode.

Get to know this subpersonality a little better. Give it some space to communicate with you. Let it express itself to you, to talk about itself. What are its feelings? Its thoughts? Let it tell you what it needs from you. When you feel ready, open your eyes and take a few minutes to write about this experience and what you know about this subpersonality.

Now close your eyes again. Find a place inside you from which you can accept this part of you . . . a place where you are willing to give it the right to exist.

Imagine that you are in a garden. It is the most beautiful garden you have ever been in. You and this subpersonality are there in this garden together. Spend some time being in this incredible place.

Look around you and explore the beauty of the garden. You and your subpersonality are alone, surrounded by nature. Walk around and visit the garden with your subpersonality. Feel the colours of the flowers; smell their fragrance. Feel the magic of this enchanted place. Together you enjoy the beauty. Be absorbed by the magic of it all.

As you keep walking you will come to the centre of the garden. There you see one rose flower unopened, on one rose bush, just in the centre of the garden. The two of you come together there and look at this unopened rose blossom. You sit down by it. As you both sit and watch, the rose begins to bloom. Very slowly, incredibly slowly, it begins to blossom. First the sepals begin to spread and the bud itself is revealed. Then the bud starts to unfold, to swell and the petals open. Little by little you and your subpersonality watch this process of life happening before you.

You see the rose slowly come to blossom fully. As it does, you realize that there is an intense fragrance emanating from it. You are both aware of this fragrance emanating from the rose and you let yourselves be pervaded by it.

Finally, shift your eyes from the rose to your subpersonality. Notice whether it is different. Be aware of the contact between you now. Interact with each other if it feels right. Say anything you want to say. There may be no need for words, you might want to interact physically. See if you can discover the quality that is trying to come through this subpersonality. What does it essentially have to contribute to you and your life?

When you feel complete, come back to this room and take a few minutes to write about your experience.

Processing the experience:
Either with partners or small groups share your experiences. Help each other to understand what it is the subpersonality needs as well as what it has to contribute. Explore: how you can give it what it needs and how it can express its essential quality. What does your experience mean in terms of your life?

Chapter 5

OUR HIDDEN STRENGTH

In the field of education the will introduces the dichotomy between discipline and permissiveness, between structure and the concept of going with the flow. There are some educators whose focus is *discipline*, who approach the whole task of education by operating as if there is a set of rules that each person must learn, and this set of rules is asserted and drummed into the young person. He is to be *taught*, conditioned and programmed to adopt an externally imposed system obediently. His own will is perceived as something to be *broken*, harnessed into socially accepted behaviours of compliance and co-operation.

With no malevolence, in fact with the best of intentions, the educator can repress the child's own power for taking initiative, constraining his natural impulse for self-regulation and direction. The result is often a repression of anger, a low self-esteem, and a dependence upon external authority with little or no ability for self-direction. Of course this dependency carries the possibility of a counter-dependency in the form of rebellion—but that is merely a reactive form of dependency.

The opposite attitude is the free style of educating, where the young person is allowed to behave as he wishes, without any limitations or constraints. Here the difficulty is, of course, that he will be ill-equipped for living in a structured society and for normal human relations. He too will be quite unable to discipline himself. Most likely he will be incapable of setting a purpose or following any given course and he may continually fall prey to his own impulses.

The attitudes outlined above towards the will of the learner are two extremes. A compromise between them will not work. It would only be a mixture of contradictory elements, bringing confusion and uncertainty in its wake. Basically our ideal should be to foster and teach the individual to learn to discipline himself—rather than enforce discipline from the outside or provide no discipline at all.

A central issue is the formation of an individual's value system. An important factor is whether the value system adopted is internalized or remains externally asserted. If the adult world *externally* regulates a child, determining and enforcing what is *right* and *wrong*, without communicating why or for what purpose, the child does not develop an *internalized* set of controls. His value system does not mature. All he is aware of is a set of rules with the 'big people' against the 'little people', with the little people abiding. The child will come to rely upon the environment to discipline and control him, without acquiring the capacity to direct and regulate himself. Often the authority figure is not consistent. The ultimate insult is for a young person to experience adults imposing discipline and rules of behaviour, while violating those same values with their own behaviour: do as I say but not as I do. Research has shown that if no *inner* value system is formed, the attitude develops that whatever one can get away with is acceptable, and that the only reason not to do certain things is that the authority may catch and punish one. On the other hand, if there are no controls or if adults provide no models, the young person is subjected to the anxiety of having to find them for himself, of feeling disorientated, and of being forced to grow up too quickly.

Roberto Assagioli described the will as the unknown factor in modern education. For him, it was the very central position of the will, as the function most directly related to the self, that is the cause for it being ignored. Perhaps the reason for its neglect lies simply in the distorted conception of the will that we all have met, the 'Victorian will'. Who has not experienced being driven by some 'should' and have not we all tried to reach our aims through force and repression? The young are often conditioned to be *good* and to behave as acculturated beings whose 'beastliness' has been subdued. This repressive effort is not true will; Assagioli's concept suggests a will that is not a rigid attitude of judgement, not a stressful discipline, not repression, but the capacity to make choices, to be responsible and to honour one's own values. Psychologist Otto Rank went as far as to say that the human being experiences his individuality in terms of his will and that his personal existence is identical with his capacity to express his will in the world.[1]

Understandably the easiest course for educators is to impose their own will on the child for the sake of order and discipline, and to guide the child implicitly to repress his own impulses. Very often this is achieved through the blackmail device of *conditional love*, i.e. capitalizing upon the child's need for love, acceptance and approval. A well-behaved child may *look like* he possesses true will, but in reality all he has is a well-functioning system of repression.

What is true will as opposed to stiff discipline? We can best understand this point by studying biological evolution. All organisms as they evolve, pass from eteronomy to autonomy. Eteronomy means having one's law outside oneself, the cause of one's movements or action being a factor other than the self, for instance as a leaf, if blown here and there by the wind. The higher on the evolutionary scale we rise, the greater the autonomy. A stone is completely eteronomous, an insect is more autonomous than a plant, and a dolphin is more autonomous than an insect. Autonomy means 'having one's law *inside* oneself', or being one's own law. It implies being a *cause*, initiating action instead of submitting to it.

We can define true will as the ability to find our own law in ourselves, therefore being able to be cause rather than effect. Autonomy comes naturally to a child as he grows and evolves, provided he has been loved and nurtured and possesses a healthy self-image. To the extent that he has experienced being lovable and worthwhile, and feels that the world is benevolent and trustworthy, he will have a solid ground to stand on, and will be able to affirm himself and to discover his own will. We only have to co-operate with the natural evolutionary process if the child's conception of himself is positive and life-affirming. We can reasonably assume that every individual possesses an inherent thrust towards greater autonomy, fuller individuality, and an increasing desire to regulate and direct himself.

A child or adolescent may express his will in its most positive forms as aggression or crude self-assertion. This is not negative in itself, for it is a step towards the development of qualities such as autonomy, the ability to risk and face danger, perseverance, the overcoming of laziness and tenacity.

For the most part aggression or assertion occur because we don't feel complete or satisfied—consequently we feel compelled to make something happen in the environment which will enable us to affirm ourselves and to become whole. We may experience a blind impulse to reach into life to get what we want. It can be a great discovery for an individual to discover his power, his possibility for having an impact, for being a cause in the universe, to be able to make his own statement in life.

However, in its first stages of development assertion is a blind and selfish impulse that can cause many difficulties to others. Those aggressive children in the class, the ones who are always in trouble and creating havoc, are often desperately seeking some way to know and prove they exist. They are simply affirming themselves in an inappropriate way, which unfortunately at times causes pain to other people.

However, if their efforts were to be perceived for what they are we would not need to counter them so strongly and with equally crude attempts at control and repression. Instead, the child should be led to see that there are other people who have their own feelings and responses. This learning may be the beginning of more mature ways of willing and relating. (The section of this book on dealing with problematic feelings can provide guidance on effective ways of approaching assertion problems.)

To understand better what the will is in its various aspects, we can envision what a child or young person would be like who possessed and demonstrated true will. What qualities and capacities would he demonstrate? What behaviours would authentic autonomy reflect? The following is a list of the main qualities and skills which are manifested in authentic volition.

Inner freedom
An individual whose will is developed has a clear perspective of the alternatives available to him and is able to choose

autonomously from among them. For example, when he watches television he is not likely to remain glued to anything that is being shown, but will be able to decide which programme to watch. He would also have the inner strength not to watch television at all and to start some other activity such as playing sport, reading a book or going to see a friend. He is interested in a variety of activities and can autonomously choose the one he prefers, independently of peer pressure or other factors. Boredom would be rare.

Inner freedom is the result of an internalized value system and gives a child the capacity to be a leader rather than a follower. If, for example, his friends want to engage in some activity which violates his value system, he would have the strength to say no, and also he would have the imagination and self-assurance necessary to propose alternative choices.

Ability to take responsibility
We have all met the child who is clearly in touch with his own preferences and knows what he likes and dislikes. This child is able to be responsible for his feelings, attitudes and behaviours and has the choice not to do what others do. He can have the courage to face anxiety and to be loyal to himself and to others. For example, if he spills some milk, he has the courage to say, 'I spilled the milk' and to take the consequences for his behaviour, rather than evading the truth.

Internalized value system
In this era of mass media, children are more exposed than ever to standardized and lowered values. Parents often express concern about this problem and wonder how they can defend their child from being absorbed by our degraded value system. A child needs the inner strength to withstand peer pressure, even at the risk of ridicule, unpopularity or threats, and to stand by his own principles. There is an urgent need today for a child to have some options and an ability to discriminate, to know which values are his own and to experience them in himself.

Self-affirmation
The self-affirming child has his own ideas and has the power to affirm and defend them. He can assert himself without seeking

the help of an authority figure. He is not the child who sits quietly without speaking up, allowing others to take the lead, the child who is frightened and unable to take initiative or make the first move in relation to other children. If he is silent, his is a *strong silence* because he has the choice to speak or not.

Capacity To Be Alone

The child who knows what he wants and is able to get it, and who is clearly conscious of his own values and preferences, is more likely to be able to be alone with himself without the compulsive need to depend on others for security, fulfilment of a task or for entertainment.

Self-discipline

A self-disciplined child is able to concentrate, to study and keep at it without outside intervention. He will complete everyday chores, such as tidying up his room, without being told to. He has the capacity to control himself in a positive way in relation to other people. He has the ability to postpone immediate gratification. For example, to save money to buy later what he *really* wants, rather than spend it to satisfy sudden impulse. He can finish a project instead of starting something else again and again, or read a book without distraction, or listen without interruption.

Courage

As is the case of many other of the traits discussed in this chapter, courage is born of a child living in a secure and nourishing environment. In such an environment he is surrounded by love but at the same time encouraged to develop the ability to take risks and face challenges bravely. There are big differences in children's ability to risk, to enter into the unknown, to try out new things and relationships, to step beyond their comfort zone. Children often find themselves in situations that are frightening to them. To give in to their fear leads to low self-esteem, to risk is a victory.

Ability to perceive the consequences of one's own actions

This ability requires the possibility to reason things out and think them through. It means freedom from compulsiveness or identification with the desires and impulses of the moment.

It is the ability to stop and put psychological distance between one's self and one's decisions and to reflect calmly upon the consequences. For example, 'If I throw the stone through the window someone might get hurt', or 'If I don't do my homework today then I won't know how to answer questions tomorrow at school'.

Good will
Recent research shows that babies, rather than being naturally selfish creatures, as many authorities believed, are naturally altruistic. These selfless tendencies, however, tend to become repressed through outer conditioning. We can be watchful of spontaneous altruistic actions in babies and children, and encourage and respect them. This attitude will later support the emergence of good will. This should not be thought of as mere affirmation, but can be coloured by the warm tones of a loving attitude. A child with a disposition to good will shows compassion for other children and will easily give up something he cherishes, a toy for instance; he will engage in acts of generosity, and will welcome the chance to take care of other children.

An Impossible Ideal?
This description of the wilful child may provoke scepticism or disbelief. I acknowledge that it is an ideal which, like all ideals, can either be a cause of frustration and unhappiness, or a source of inspiration. The qualities and skills I have described are not an impossible dream. They are present in various degrees and combinations in all children.

It is important to have this in mind when we educate. Our work will be as effective as the *vision* we hold, and if we ignore these possibilities they will be less likely to manifest.

There are three major ways for the educator to facilitate the emergence and development of the will in those he educates: by being a living example, by perceiving and encouraging the will when it is emerging, and by the structured use of experiential work designed to foster its evolution.

To be a living example
The educator himself can be a living embodiment of that

which he seeks to foster and develop in the young. If we embody true will our attitudes and qualities will be contagious. We cannot avoid being a model from which children will learn. The young often learn unconsciously and spontaneously, by imitation, without the need for explicit guidance.

Mature self-assertion, persistence, willingness to risk and honesty to acknowledge mistakes, good will, concentration, self-discipline, the more a child will see these qualities, the more he will absorb them and be inspired by them. On the other hand, children who meet assertion of will through control, repression and psychological or even physical violence, will also be prone to be and act as they have been shown.

A few examples of an embodiment or skilful evocation of the will would be:

— an educator patiently helping a child to see the consequences of his behaviour.

— a teacher guiding a child step by step in the learning of a new skill and allowing him to learn at his own pace.

— a parent reacting with loving firmness to his child's misbehaviour, without condemnation or authoritarian punishment.

— an interpersonal conflict being resolved by each party finding a way to honour his own values without negating the other's point of view.

— an educator giving up a structured programme when it is not appropriate, for the sake of the class.

— an educator consciously seeking the opinion of the more introverted class members.

— a parent giving his child alternatives from which to choose, according to what matters most to him.

— an educator explaining why a certain behaviour in the classroom is not acceptable, rather than just asserting rules.

— an educator guiding the class to create its operating principles rather than imposing a pre-conditioned set of regulations.

— a parent giving his child the opportunity to say 'no', and not needing to assert himself against it.

— an educator giving class members opportunities for independence, without stepping in at difficult moments.

— an adult trusting a child to work alone without constantly checking his progress.
— a demonstration of concentrated thinking and an ability to withstand distractions.

Perception of emerging will
If the educator holds an inspired vision, in this instance, a vision of the potential for will and autonomy in the young, he creates the psychological space for it to emerge. Our awareness is limited by our ability to perceive and our perception must be sufficiently open to seeing what we *will* to see. If we as educators recognize some inkling of true will manifesting, we can point it out to the child and reinforce it rather than ignore it or even discourage it.

When we are confronted with the more crude and distorted attempts of the young, our usual stance is to reject or seek to control these behaviours. Instead, we could acknowledge and validate them. This does not mean that we have to sacrifice our principles or codes of good conduct, but rather that we see the totality of what is happening and do not react only to surface events. The needed perception is one of *bifocal vision*: there is the emerging, if unevolved, affirmation of self, *and* there is possibly unacceptable behaviour. We must recognize that a child or adolescent is not *only* his behaviour. He is also a being that is seeking autonomy.

Most importantly, whenever we see courage, self-discipline, perseverance, good will or skilful assertion occurring, we should shine the light of our attention by affirming these aspects and giving them space. To make explicit to a child our positive perception of his emergence will nourish him as surely as water nourishes a plant. To notice and respond when, in spite of peer pressure, an adolescent is taking responsibility for his actions and honouring his values gives him the impetus to continue. To acknowledge an act of courage, to reward thorough and persistent work, to praise and reinforce healthy wilful behaviour, stimulates these qualities. I have noticed skilful educators subtly creating *teaching points* from their students' demonstrations of true will.

Experiential work to foster the will
Every exercise we do, or every structure we provide, stimulates

the will, because focus, patience and decisiveness are needed to implement it. However, we can explore the will specifically by doing exercises which are designed to foster it. Class projects may be done on the will and its aspects. By coming to understand it, to recognize its value, to play with its qualities, to 'advertise' its advantages without imposing them, we lead the child or young person towards a deeply gratifying experience.

EXERCISES

CONCENTRATION AND OBSERVATION: CAN YOU?

The ability to observe, focus and sustain concentration is of unquestionable value for education. This exercise provides an enjoyable way of training the will through focused attention and concentration. It teaches a skill which is useful for any topic of study and promotes the potential for detailed awareness of the activity in hand.

Age: seven–adult
Time: 30 minutes
Equipment: Ten to forty small objects of various kinds, sizes and colours. For example: a pen, stamp, piece of fruit, toy car, fork, rubber, paper clip, sponge, bar of soap, balloon, crayon, marble, shoe, book, glass, tissue, etc.
Exercise:
Let the participants look for two minutes at the objects as they are laid out. Just look, don't touch or pick them up, and do not talk during these minutes.

Cover the objects with a towel or sheet. Each participant says what objects he remembers under the towel. The educator counts how many things each child remembered. For older people, ask each participant to write down what he remembers under the sheet.

BUILDING OUR ABILITY TO WILL

Everyday life provides a rich field of opportunities for learning to use the will. Through choosing and honouring that choice in simple ways we can train our ability to will. This exercise allows the participant to create the experience of willing in a simple and effective way.

Age: five to adult
Time: determined by the chosen activity
Exercise:
For younger children the action chosen needs to be simple and quickly done, and possibly one of building a good habit like brushing the teeth daily. The choice of action need not be extravagant. For adolescents or adults, the choice of activity should be made by the participant (not imposed from the outside) and should not be one where strong emotions are involved. Examples could be: keeping a journal, writing a letter, ten minutes of physical exercise, or doing something one is slightly afraid of.

Choose the activity to be done each day and clearly define that activity and why you want to do it. Then as each day comes make sure you honour your choice. You may want to keep a record of each time you do it.

WHAT DOES IT MEAN TO CHOOSE?

We make choices every moment but are seldom *consciously* making those choices. Life is the best laboratory for learning to make the *process* of willing conscious. Our best tool is awareness and introspection. To watch ourselves as we make a choice, to experience fully what happens *inside* as we carry it out, and to be aware of the result of our actions, can enable us to employ our will more skilfully and to recognize the immense power that we as individuals hold. This simple exercise is designed to create the opportunity for small acts of will to be actualized.

Age: ten–adult
Time: 15 minutes for the exercise
         30 minutes for processing the exercise
Exercise:
I invite you to do an exercise with me now, but I would like you to make the choice to do it or not. So would you each decide if you are willing to do this exercise.

Look around the room and think of all the possible things you might choose to do in this room right now. (Obviously things that are not harmful to yourself, other people or the environment.) Here are some examples: open the window, write your name on the board, move your chair to the front of the room, tidy your desk, say hello to a friend, untie your shoe laces, stand on your chair, tell someone you like them—whatever. Your possibilities are unlimited and do not have to be significant or important. Just explore all of the many alternative actions you could choose.

Now choose one of those alternatives and go and do it. (Educator: allow sufficient time for participants to carry out their acts of will, about five minutes.)

Without talking to others, go back to considering again all the possible alternatives for things you could choose to do right now in this room. Only this time as you reflect, be aware of what is going on *inside* you as you explore. How do you choose? What do you feel? How is your body? What is the process that happens as you make a choice?

Now make the choice to do something and observe what happens as you make it. Choose again and then go and do it. (Educator: again allow sufficient time for participants to carry out their acts of will.)

Now, again without talking to anyone, think of one more act of will you could choose here in the room. Consider again your alternatives. Now choose *not* to do it. Experience what that is like for you.

Processing the experience:
In small groups, or the large group, discuss what it is like to make a choice. How do you choose? What is the process you went through as you explored alternatives? What kinds of consequences did you think about? Was there an element of risk? Were you free to change your mind or not?

I SHOULD BUT I COULD
As we all have experienced how difficult it is to accomplish something when we are pushing, making an effort and forcing ourselves to do it, perhaps we can transform this repressive way of doing things into a possibility which contains freedom of choice. Any time we feel 'I must' or 'I have to' we rob ourselves of the healthy use of our will. To use our will in a forceful coercive way only causes us to resist and rebel, whereas if we always have the possibility of yes or no (which is in fact at every moment true) we have a greater potential for actually doing what we will to do. This exercise provides the experience of the difference between Victorian will and true will.

Age: fourteen–adult
Time: one hour
Exercise:
Find a partner to work with. Sit facing your partner.

Now each participant write across the top of a sheet of paper 'I should' and make a list of all the things you should do or be. Make as extensive a list as possible. The things your head tells you that you should do, the things your parents tell you, your teacher, your friends—things you *should* do or be, from brushing your teeth every morning to keeping your room tidy to always being nice to people to being a good person, being popular with your friends, going to church, studying hard and getting good marks—the lot.

If you find you have an 'I shouldn't', try to find the positive counterpart to it. For example: 'I shouldn't smoke' to 'I should only do what's healthy for my body.'

Now exchange lists with your partner. Each of you will have a turn. One partner at a time read out your partner's list to him in this way:
'You should _____.' (Partner hearing it respond with NO.)
'You should _____.' (Partner hearing it respond with NO.)
Go through the entire list this way.
Now switch and the second partner read the other person's list to him, in the same way.

Now we will each have a turn to read to our partner his list of shoulds again, only this time when you hear the 'should', change it to 'I could'. For example: 'You *should* be a loving person.' 'I *could* be a loving person.' (And I have a choice.) As you say 'I could and I have a choice' allow yourself to feel as much as possible that you actually do have a choice.

Now switch and go through the other person's list in the same way.

Processing the experience:
Discuss with your partner: What was it like to say no to your shoulds? Could you actually feel that you did have a choice? Why is a should not really a choice? And a could is? Is there freedom in having choices?

REACHING OUR GOALS
Having the ability to *stay with* a chosen aim or goal until completion requires perseverance in the face of distractions.

We are easily deferred unless we can strongly visualize the goal and the positive benefits of reaching that goal. This requires the *strength* of will to persist and be one-pointed, as well as the *skilful will* to maintain the vision of our goal. The purpose of this exercise is to develop an ideal model of our potential with the aid of guided imagery.*

Age: fourteen–adult

Time: 20 minutes for exercise

20 minutes for exercise

30 minutes for processing the experience

Exercise:

Find a comfortable body position, relax, and breathe deeply for a few moments. We will be doing an exercise which helps us to envision ourselves achieving something that really matters to us.

Get in touch with or think about something that is important for you to do in your life, a priority or aim you have, a goal you sincerely wish to achieve. Take some time to get in touch with this.

Now allow an image or a symbol to appear in your mind's eye that is related to or symbolic of this chosen goal. Take your time and don't push. Do not judge or censor your images. Allow that image to become more vivid and clear.

Now imagine that this symbol is far away from you, on top of a hill. Take as much time as you need to see this symbol clearly on top of a hill in the distance. Imagine too, that you are standing on a straight road, leading from where you are to the top of the hill. Again, take some time to see this road and yourself on it.

You are going to travel this straight road to the top of the hill to reach your purpose. You can feel determination and energy to reach this goal. It is important to you. Let yourself be filled with the strong will to reach that purpose.

However, imagine that on the two sides of the road leading to your purpose are all *your* distractions to it—all the things that will try to stop you from getting there. There could be all kinds of obstacles to deflect you from reaching the top—scaring you, discouraging you, making you doubt your goal, causing you to wonder if your goal is really worthwhile and

*This exercise is adapted from *What We May Be* by Piero Ferrucci (Turnstone Press, 1982).

so on. Just pay attention to what obstacles you see or find as you begin to travel this journey.

You are walking that road now, *and* you keep going. You keep travelling and honouring that straight road to your chosen purpose. And soon you will reach the top and you can feel that you are capable of reaching the top. Your strength and determination to be true to yourself is constantly with you.

Once you have reached the top of the hill, and your goal, spend some time just enjoying being there and experiencing mastery. You have reached your image and purpose! You made it. You may want to interact with the symbol in whatever way feels right or you may just want to be there, having made it.

Processing the experience:
Come back and write a little about your experience. Remember it and record it in as much detail as possible. Break into small groups to share your purpose or goal and what this experience was like for you. Define for yourself what your obstacles were and how you felt about them. If you did not make it to the top, share with your group members what stopped you and explore what you can do about that.

As a group, look at what it means to reach a chosen purpose and what is required of us in order not to become distracted.

EXAMPLES OF WILL

Studying the biographies of individuals who clearly and successfully demonstrated true will can be both educational and stimulating. The class could choose known people who have expressed will to its fullest and research the lives of these *ideal models*. This exercise or project can enable young people to grasp and recognize more fully the value of the will and the positive effects it can bring to people's lives, the sense of purpose and fulfilment it evokes.
Age: twelve–adult
Time: to be determined by the educator.
Equipment: Articles or biographies of chosen individuals embodying Will.
Exercise:
Spend as much time as appropriate discussing the lives of the

chosen individuals and determining what qualities they expressed; what they achieved in their life and how their will enabled them to do so; what inspired them to use their will so effectively; how these attributes can exist in a young person's life; and what that would look like.

To follow, each participant could choose an act of will they would like to make in their life, and plan a programme of how they could actualize it.

YES, I CAN!

A successful act of will contains within it a model of how to use the will effectively. Every young person has at some time in their life made a choice, taken a step, affirmed himself in some way. To become conscious of the dynamics of this successful act of will can energize and inspire the individual to do it again. Every adolescent has *something* worthwhile which he sincerely wills to achieve. That *something* may be a small step, like remembering to tell his mother what time he will be home from school, or a larger dream to actualize, like learning to speak up in class. This exercise can enable the adolescent to explore *how* it might be possible for him to actualize his will.

Age: fourteen–adult

Time: 45 minutes for exercise

45 minutes for processing the experience

Exercise:

Find a comfortable body position, relax, and breathe deeply for a moment or two. Now recall a time from your past, in your life, when you felt you used your will, or made a choice, or took a step in a good and successful way. Take a moment to let that experience come into focus, to let it emerge. It may have been a very simple small step that you took, or it may have been a very big and significant time.

In your imagination right now, let your memory of this experience come alive. Make it as real as you possibly can for yourself, right now. What was happening in this experience? What were you doing? Who were you with? What were you wearing? How did you look? What were you feeling at the time? What thoughts, considerations and evaluations were going through your mind? How did your body feel in this willing act? What was the quality of the experience for you? What was the result of the experience? What changes did it bring to your life?

Take a few minutes to write down what this act of will was like for you.

Now break into small groups of three or four and share your experiences. Together try to define the qualities that were in your successful acts of will, the common points of your different experiences, and what was most important for all of you.

Let's all close our eyes and go back inside ourselves for a few minutes. Get in touch with something in your life that you would like to choose to do or achieve. It can be a small immediate step you want to take in your life right now, or a bigger, long-range decision that feels right for you. Take time to define that for yourself. See if you feel that you are able to make that choice and do it for yourself right now. If not, ask yourself: 'What is it that stops me from doing it?' 'What blocks me?' 'What do I need in order to say, yes, I can?'

Remember what it was like in your experience of successfully willing. How can you use what you learned in that previous experience for this one? Be as detailed as possible. Take some time now to write about this.

Processing the experience:
Again break into the same small group as before and share this part of your experience. Group members should help each other to discover the means to carry out their chosen action.

Chapter 6

ADOLESCENT IDENTITY STRUGGLES

Adolescence is a time of stress and turmoil and is characterized by several familiar crises, the outcome of which play a major role in the formation of the adult personality. These are: the conflict between feelings and mind; emerging sexuality; independence from parents; the formation of self-image, identity, a framework of values and a cohesive world-view. These crises, which have their roots in early childhood, generally appear in adolecence, although occasionally they do not emerge until later in life. The emotional intensity of adolescent problems deserves our compassionate understanding. Fortunately during this period most young people are both interested in and willing to take increasing responsibility for their growth process.

The Conflict Between Feelings and Mind
This can be a frequent cause of stress, particularly for adolescents, but it has been discussed in depth in the previous chapter on the development of the mind. It is important to say here that if this duality is not resolved during adolescence, its effects can persist throughout adult life.

Emerging Sexuality
In this phase of life the body changes radically: genital puberty floods the body and imagination with many conflicting impulses, as intimacy with the opposite sex suggests itself. In puberty and throughout adolescence sexual awareness increases and emotional life deepens through the emergence of

sexual energy. The body is defined in new ways via its relationship to the feelings, bringing with it tumultuous emotional upheavals. Relationships with the opposite sex can pervade consciousness during this period. Acceptance by the opposite sex is crucial for many young people and this overriding concern often interferes with their education.

Some major issues include the meaning of male/female roles and the influence of cultural conditioning upon these roles, what sexual behaviour is appropriate, and questions of identity in the eyes of the opposite sex. Often an adolescent will systematically experiment by adopting different subpersonalities, for example, the tomboy, the flirt, the liberated woman or man, the rebel, the little child, etc. and will then assimilate the essence of the psychological states contained within the enacted roles. This testing process further elaborates the differentiation of emotions. As adolescence is a time of such experimentation, perceived successes and failures are always present, along with their accompanying emotional reactions.

An adolescent may temporarily over-identify with the clique or crowd of which he has chosen to be a part, to the point at which there is an apparent loss of individuality. Falling in love, at this stage, is not primarily a sexual matter, it is an attempt to establish identity by projecting a self-image and having it reflected back and gradually clarified. Through these processes a sexual identity is formed, the effects of which may be life-lasting.

Independence and Separation From Parents

During this period one can observe a curious contrast in a young man; on the one hand, he opens himself to all influences; he is sensitive, receptive to every current. On the other hand, he is suspicious and rebellious against interference on the part of others, especially against those who are naturally inclined to exert that influence, namely his parents and educators. He keenly feels the need for independence and liberty and often demands it in an aggressive way. This urge is deeply justified: the young adolescent must form his personality through experiences of all kinds, following an inner line of development. Every unjustified interference, every attempt at guidance, every pressure intended to mould him according to other people's views and desires are felt by him to be violation of, a menace to, his free and spontaneous transformation.[1]

Assagioli is referring here to the classic conflict between the generations, which may emerge with more or less acuity and occasional violence. There is the tension-creating struggle between adults and the young, but more specifically between parents and children. This is an aspect of the wider conflict between authority and control on the one hand and freedom and independence on the other.

Alongside emerging sexuality is the age-old process of ending the dependency relationship with one's parents and authority figures. Few of us have forgotten the difficulty of this separation, nor the ambivalence that comes with it. I am frequently moved by the 'half child/half adult' of many young people. At times they may have an unconscious wish to remain a child, safe and protected by parental figures, clinging to the known, familiar dependency of early childhood. But at other moments they wrench away, rejecting their parental figures. Often an adolescent will rely on his peer group for support to enable him to let go and to rebel.

Again many alternative ways of feeling, thinking and behaving may be explored and, often in order to make the needed separation, rebellion becomes a healthy necessity. Parents, and their way of being and living, will invariably be judged as wrong and unacceptable. Rejection is followed by the temporary adoption of polar opposite values, but this may be only short-lived. An adolescent will strive to experience his identity as distinct from his parents. If we as educators take these explorations personally, we may interfere with the necessary process of the adolescent finding his way; especially if we wield authority and power to force compliance to an acceptable norm. Many parents with whom I have worked experienced comfort and relief when reassured of the temporary nature of this rebellion and found it effective to give space for experimentation. It is a period when children may appear to have lost their love for their parents, and it will seem to the parents that they can never 'get it right'. Perhaps they should surrender their need to. This separation is closely linked with the establishment of the young person's self-image and identity, which is explored in the next section.

Self-Image and Identity

The formation of self-image is based primarily on the adolescent's earlier childhood experience of two potent forces, love and will, which are determined primarily by parents and educators. By love I mean an individual's experience of himself as being lovable, his basic trust in the fundamental 'alrightness' of life, his perception of his environment's willingness to nurture and support him, and his capacity for intimacy. Being loved and feeling lovable is an unconscious motivating force which consistently determines much of human behaviour. Furthermore this condition determines our ability to love others and to express love. The drive for love and unity is universal, forming the *ground* upon which a child stands.

Negative behaviour patterns are often formed. For some the pattern is one of being very dependent, obedient and conformist, always trying hard to please. For others, who experience the world as a negative and threatening place in which caution is needed, the pattern may be one of control and manipulation. Both are doing whatever it takes to get their needs for love and security met. Occasionally, we find extreme neediness and an inability to get enough affirmation. For such a child there is a *hole in the bucket* which never *allows* the experience of being lovable. The degree to which we perceive ourselves as lovable is directly proportional to our sense of self-worth and self-image. Though in reality it has very little to do with our nature, it will have a dramatic impact. The firmness of this *ground* on which we stand obviously affects how we approach the world in many ways, particularly in our interpersonal relationships.

If a child's ground is unstable, it is very difficult to express his will, to assert himself, and to become autonomous. It may feel too dangerous and threatening for him to affirm himself, even to the extreme of feeling that his whole world might collapse. Due to earlier experiences of *conditional* love, healthy self-assertion may have been repressed. For example, parents may have threatened to withdraw their love unless aggressive behaviour was controlled. Another example is the widespread social conditioning that *nice girls aren't assertive,* but soft and sweet.

A child may be confronted with a conflict of conformity versus self-assertion. Although he may be unable to articulate them, these sorts of questions arise, 'Should I conform in order to get my needs met or can I risk asserting who I am?' 'What will happen if I establish my boundaries and identity?' 'Will I be accepted or not?' 'Is my behaviour an expression of me or of what the environment wants?' 'Who am I when I assert myself?' Finding the answers to these questions can be confusing.

We may also find the opposite behaviour in the adolescent who resists control and rebels. He is unconsciously using his 'no' as a negative assertion of his will. He will set rigid boundaries of self in order to find autonomy. Whilst 'no' is a form of assertion, a self-image formed of negation is lacking in substance. Instead, a defensive structure is built up through which little can penetrate. There can be a pervasive withholding of expression, of feelings, needs and opinions which further inhibits the formation of self-image.

Research has shown that a child who succeeds every time he asserts himself develops without a sense of boundary, without a clear definition between himself and the world, and may eventually have psychotic tendencies. On the other hand the child who is never allowed healthy self-assertion will tend towards neurosis; his self-image is externally conditioned and defined. It is acceptable, even healthy, for a young person to assert himself by pushing against the environment *and* this should not mean he is unlovable.

A sense of identity is crucial to the feeling of being alive, and the search for identity is an important dynamic of adolescence. We will see later that identity is more than a conglomeration of current psychosocial traits, that there is in each individual an 'I', an observing centre of awareness and volition which transcends psychosocial identity. In the process of establishing this transcending identity, an individual must go through a period of living his psychosocial identity. It is at the psychosocial level that an adolescent's relationship with his peer group takes on supreme significance and sometimes obsession. The finding of a subculture with which he can identify becomes important. Adolescents are deeply concerned with how they appear in the eyes of others as compared with what they feel they are. They seek congruence between these two perceptions. For example, though I was elected 'class queen' for several years, and was popular with teachers and students alike, *inside* I was haunted with feelings of inadequacy and unworthiness. Identity is the accrued confidence that comes when a sense of personal continuity is consistent with an individual's fantasy of how others perceive him.

An adolescent may experiment with many different roles in his unconscious search for identity. People with whom he comes into contact may be unwittingly selected to play arbitrary roles. As a young person relies upon peers for support in order to let go of parents, he will identify temporarily with new and different ways of being and relating. Although they seem permanent, these roles are transitory, but they do contribute to an eventual identity formation. Within this context subcultures or cliques form. These groups may consist of anything from a few friends to the extreme of the recent macro-cultures of punks and 'skins'. Their behaviour becomes stereotyped and their ideals crystallized, and the false sense of security that they provide supports their members through the confusion of this period. These groups carry with them incredible rituals and ways of dressing, for example the Saturday afternoon parade on London's Kings Road.

Conformity brings solidarity but along with that comes a sometimes cruel intolerance of differences and sharp divisions between inclusion and exclusion. It is important to recognize, even if we do not condone it, that these unattractive manifestations may be a necessary defence against loss of a sense of identity. The *content* of this subculture should not concern us; its importance lies in the process, which provides the opportunity for the young to experiment with, experience, and express a variety of psychosocial conditions.

Self-identification

It is not until around the ages of sixteen to eighteen that a sense of true self-identity may begin to emerge. Until this time the growth and development of the three major functions, body, feelings and mind, predominate and this process should not be inhibited, nor a search for identity encouraged too early. Educator Rudolf Steiner particularly stressed that we should not rush the development of the 'transpersonal domain' in the child, but rather that he must be allowed to develop his personality properly if he is to become a well-founded, capable and entirely human individual. Steiner wrote:

The growing child is by no means a 'self' in the usual sense of the word until he passes through puberty. Not until then does his selfhood unfold. Then and only then can he be regarded as having at his disposal a self which he can express.[2]

Psychosynthesis also emphasizes allowing the full unfoldment of the three major functions of the personality *before* encouraging the adolescent to discover that who he actually is is more than his body, his feelings, or his mind. He has a body, he has feelings and he has a mind, which are rich and precious tools for life, but who is he? And what exactly do we mean by self? As I implied in the previous section there *is* an element within us which is permanent, although everything about us changes. Body experience changes, feelings come and go, thoughts flow by, but *someone* remains to experience this flow. This is our 'self', our core, our essential beingness.

One of the basic tenets of psychosynthesis is: 'We are dominated by everything with which our self is identified. We can dominate and control everything from which we dis-identify ourselves.'[3] It is through this curious process of dis-identification that a true experience of 'I' or identity can be obtained. Early experiences of this 'I' or personal self are extremely important. Until they happen, an adolescent cannot experience himself as separate and distinct from his many varied and conflictual parts—be it body sensations, mixed emotions, mental constructs, or any of the painful elements within developmental issues previously mentioned. This *point* of self-awareness acts as a unifying and integrating centre. It is 'the conductor of our orchestra' and is our first step towards an experience of the transpersonal realm. If we accept that this is so, what is the process by which this experience can be evoked in young people?

As a child grows, he is *identified* with whatever phase of development he is in. If he is experiencing a strong feeling, like despair, he *is* that despair; if feeling loving, he *is* that love; if angry, he *is* that anger; if a moment of insecurity is present, he *is* that insecurity, strength, self-confidence, wilfulness or fear. He is whatever the content of his experience might be. This also occurs mentally, with beliefs, opinions or thoughts. Whatever an individual is identified with consumes his consciousness at that moment, dominates it, and controls it, limiting his awareness and perception. It blocks the possibility and availability of any other feeling, sensation or thought. This is the nature of identification, and in itself there is nothing wrong with it. One way we grow is through identifying with a psychological element, such as courage, and by the process assimilating it into our own repertoire. Through this process also we can differentiate into subtler and more complex levels which give us a more refined capacity to experience life. Psychosynthesis recognizes identification as a necessary stage, but does not see it as an end point and the time inevitably comes when identification is limiting.

We *dis*-identify by observing. Instead of being unconsciously lost in and absorbed by whatever sensations, feelings and thoughts that are occurring, we objectively observe without interpreting, judging, analysing or trying to change— we accept what is. The result of cultivating the ability to observe liberates us from the domination and control of psychological elements.

The first field of observation is that of sensations produced by bodily conditions. Physical experience is constantly changing, we may be healthy or ill, tense or relaxed, tired or rested.

The second field of inner observation is that of feelings and emotions. The process of observing feelings is especially difficult for adolescents, but gaining psychological distance from the intense swings of emotional life is essential. Given the sometimes negative reactions to their own development, and the various crises of adolescence, it is a great relief to adolescents if they can discover that their identity is more than their feelings. An adolescent needs to cultivate the choice of whether to be fully immersed in his emotions and controlled by them *or* the inner freedom to identify with a part of himself *or* to step back from that part if it limits him or is not appropriate.

The third field of observation is that of mental activity. This involves a process of *watching* thoughts pass in and out of the mind, in the way one might watch the random flutterings of a butterfly. The objective observation of the mind's wanderings inevitably produces a sense of dis-identification from psychological activities.

The observer will become aware that he can not only

observe but also influence the spontaneous flow and regulation of psychological states. This corresponds to the concept of *personal responsibility*, the idea that we can take responsibility for, and control in a regulatory sense, the direction of our life. The freedom to choose what we want to be, or to choose appropriate responses, comes in a large measure through *dis-identification* from all that which is not the essential self and through *identification* with a deeper centre of being.

The Adoption of a World View and Values

Young people are prone to experiences which could be termed transpersonal or spiritual. Especially, though not only, during adolescence they may have what Maslow termed *peak experiences* of a transpersonal nature, which will be experienced primarily through their feelings. These experiences often include a greatly increased appreciation of beauty and nature, a true recognition of the inter-connectedness of all life, an awareness of human interdependence and the value of loving one's fellow man. These experiences often bring with them a sense of the meaning and purpose inherent in life. This may lead to a period of philosophical interest with ponderings on the existence of God and what this might mean to them. These profound experiences will be explored further in the chapter on the transpersonal.

Such visions may conflict sharply with the young person's current experience of everyday life. A common element of peak experiences is an awareness of the magnificent potential of humanity, and of the perfection of all life. This greatly contrasts with the existence of war and starvation, the knowledge that their personality is imperfect, and the reality of social problems. This duality leads to psychological dissonance and a sense of meaninglessness, impotency, and despair. An adolescent's vision is greater than his ability to live or express that vision. His still-developing personality seems woefully inadequate to cope.

This crisis of duality, coupled with their sometimes potent anger towards adults for creating many of their problems, can cause adolescents to lash out and reject authority. Needless to say, their anger is seldom appropriately received by those supposedly more mature and we see the endless chain of difficulties between the generations. Many distorted behaviours may emerge, all the way from rebellious and destructive acts, to 'dropping out', or fanaticism and excessive idealism. As adults we may lack grace in our understanding and acceptance of such reactions. We often blindly expect our young to perceive us with a certain respect or adoration, without acknowledging our part in current social concerns.

Not only must an adolescent come to terms with today's long list of social concerns, but also with his own emotional response to these issues and the impact they may have upon his future. We do little or nothing to equip them to deal with these international, social and domestic crises which range from family problems, the breakdown of the nuclear family, and living with excessive crime and violence, to unemployment and poor prospects of future employment, environmental pollution, and nuclear destruction. Surely, if we adults have not yet found a way to solve these problems, we can at least have compassion with an adolescent who questions his future and our values. The primary problem I have found in this area is the dismissive attitude of authority in the adult world and the young person's deep emotional response to this attitude.

If an adolescent's pain related to these conditions and his other accompanying emotions are not allowed to surface and be worked through, they will inevitably be suppressed. Some unconscious reactions I have seen in adolescents are despair, hopelessness, meaninglessness, fear, anger, rage and guilt that they cannot do or are not doing more. These are not neurotic tendencies but compassionate responses, which arise from the unconscious perception of human interconnectedness and are an indication of a more global awareness at work. If we repress this awareness, we render ourselves impotent and unable to face life creatively. The effects may be alienation, closed hearts and a narrowing of vision to selfish concerns. Repression is never successful, as feelings will surface in other guises, such as the self-destructiveness of drugs or alcohol, the nihilism of youth today, or the desperate pursuit of pleasure. We must not ignore the necessity to work together actively with the young on their valid concerns.

Out of all this confusion emerges the individual's world view, his system of beliefs, and his perception of reality. An adolescent must tenaciously grasp his idealistic sense of what the world is about and not be threatened by any suggestions that shake the foundations of his paradigm. His need to make order of apparent chaos may cause him to go one of two ways: one of these is to develop an excessively idealistic world view, which leads to a rigid, uncompromising, moral and ethical framework. Of course, his disillusionment and disappointment will be frequent, for neither he nor others could possibly live up to this elevated model. Frustration becomes his way of life. I have worked with adolescents who aggressively despise themselves and the world for failing to manifest an ideal world. Excessive and relentless perfectionism lead to despair and sometimes self-destructive behaviour. When we examine young people who have gone in this direction, we often find among the negative elements some very positive qualities. These comprise the increasing acquisition of self-consciousness, the potential of a healthy idealism or vision of life, the possibility of deep and heartful love, religious sentiment, enthusiasm, and compassionate humanitarian self-assertion.

The other direction that the adolescent might take is into his own existential crisis. Here despair and existential anxiety reign. It is a crisis which challenges the very meaning of life and human existence. It is the experience of emptiness, meaninglessness, and deep lack of fulfilment. Those who have experienced it speak of an existential vacuum, an endless void which has no hope, light or potential for change. 'What's it (life) all for?' 'What's the point?' 'Who cares?' 'It doesn't really matter'. These are frequently heard comments from our young today. I once saw my sixteen-year-old step-daughter smoking and asked her how she felt about the health hazards of smoking. Her response still haunts me: 'It doesn't really matter—the world could be blown up tomorrow and if it isn't, I could be murdered on the streets any time—so who cares about smoking?'

The behaviour which may result from the depth of such unaddressed despair, found in both the crisis of duality and the existential crisis, can be severely damaging to young people and their future. They may permanently harm themselves. They also may have little respect or appreciation of the positive potential contained in life; a lack of understanding and appreciation of the rights of others, a heightened arrogance covering deep feelings of inferiority; and uncertainty leading to a retreat from both society and reality. We may find them attracted to the obscure counter cultures of darkness and negativity. Many have a severe preoccupation with death and subsequent depression, sometimes leading to suicide. Statistics tell us that adolescent suicide has dramatically increased in the Western world in recent years. The quest for the meaning of being human is lost.

Without creative and healthy means for resolving these painful issues, without practical tools for acknowledging and directly confronting their dilemma, our youth will often turn to alcohol and drugs in a desperate attempt to escape. If we explored the background of kids who take this route we would be surprised by what 'normal' people they actually are—what 'normal' homes they come from, what 'normal' parents they have, what a 'normal' upbringing they have experienced. They are seldom deprived children.

I personally have seen many educators sigh and give up with these adolescents; the problem is too big, too insurmountable, too time-consuming even to think about. We must think; we must feel with them, and put ourselves in their shoes. Perhaps we must also cry with them, as their pain is ours. To turn our hearts away from them is to deny the existence of the future. Surprisingly enough, once the adolescent's pain is acknowledged, accepted and met, dramatic changes begin to happen almost at once. It is neither too big nor too late.

Both the crisis of duality and the existential crisis require from us an attitude of profound understanding, respect, and tolerance. We must acknowledge that their experience is valid, although perhaps it is not the only possibility. It is only by affirming the adolescent's experience as what *is* true right now for him, that we create the climate for it to be transcended. Our formula of 'recognition, acceptance—containment, expression or transformation' for working with these powerful feelings is usually the most effective means of dealing with both these crises.

Work with adolescents is a process to be lived with and consciously and continuously confronted. It is not alleviated with a few nice words and understanding statements; but rather requires intelligent and compassionate action. The specific transformation techniques mentioned earlier are the best way to begin, and the solution lies in dis-identification and the inclusion of the transpersonal domain.

EXERCISES

IDENTITIES THAT DEFINE WHO WE ARE

To the extent that we identify with a role, a particular way of being or behaviour, we may be limited by that identification. The *identities* that we have both serve us and limit us. They serve us by giving us a vehicle through which to express ourselves. They limit us by excluding other possibilities of feeling and behaviour. Identifications are not *bad* in themselves. The RISK lies in *unconsciously* LOSING ourselves in them.

This exercise has the purpose of facilitating recognition of how we define ourselves and developing the ability to observe our various identities. This expanded awareness enables us to act responsibly and to make choices as to how we behave in any given situation of life.

Age: fourteen–adult
Time: 45 minutes for the exercise
Equipment: Writing materials.
Exercise:

Take a moment to allow your body to relax. Now ask yourself the question: 'Who am I?' Write down several answers without much thinking. If you have any difficulty in getting an answer, just close your eyes, ask the question again and see what emerges. Then pick the five most significant answers and write each one on a slip of paper.

Now go through your slips of paper and number them 1 to 5 on the back, in order of importance to you. Number 1 is the answer that is least important to you; number 5 is the most meaningful, has the most vitality, and seems to be closer to who you *really* are. When you have ordered them turn them over so that number 1 is on top.

Now we will ask ourselves a series of questions related to those answers. (Educator: write the questions on the board and run through the first series with the participants verbally.) Go separately through each slip of paper, answering all the questions for each one. The answers should be written down.

QUESTIONS:
1. What do I get from having this identity/role?
2. How does this identity/role limit me?
3. What would it be like to let go of it?

Now symbolically let go of that identity/role by affirming: *'I am not this and I am willing to let go of it.'* Make a symbolic getsure of putting it aside. Remember you can always come back to this identity/role later. Spend a few minutes with each one.

After you have let go of each identity/role, be aware of what remains: it is *you*, your essence, your true self. Spend some time realizing this fact.

Share your experience with your partner.

Follow sharing in partners with large-group sharing. Points to cover with the larger group are:

It is important to have the choice to let go of an identity or role. This does not mean that we *have to* but we want the freedom of choice whenever possible.

You might also want to be aware of what you need to do or have in order to allow yourself to let go.

If there was an identity that you were not willing to let go of right now, perhaps it is appropriate *not* to let go. Having that identity or role may be necessary for your process right now and it may be in tune with expressing your Self.

Ultimately, all the contents, identities or roles are not really who we are. We are a Self.

THREAD OF CONTINUITY

It can be both relieving and liberating to experience a thread of continuity throughout our life, especially at time of great change and turmoil. We have a past, live in the present, and can foresee a future. Yet throughout these various stages of life, there is some aspect of us that remains the same. Ultimately we are the same self that we were as a baby, a young child, older child and now finally adolescents or adults. Experiencing this *sameness* can provide us with a sense of continuity and increase our sense of identity.

Age: fourteen–adult
Time: 20 minutes for the exercise
        30 minutes for processing the experience

Exercise:

Sit in a comfortable position, relax and quietly experience your breath—slowly inhaling and exhaling. Tune in to your 'here and now' experience. What are you experiencing right now? *Who* is having this experience? Just get a sense of that . . . I am experiencing . . .

Now I'll ask you to go back into your childhood. Allow a memory from your childhood to emerge. It can be any memory of any age. It may be a certain period from childhood, like when you started school or moved to a new city. Remember that experience, the environment, smells, sights, voices and sounds. What people were around you?

Ask yourself: *who* is experiencing this? Who was a child? Experience this sense of *I*-ness, of me-ness.

Now go to a later memory you have, one from early adolescence, or late childhood. Again allow any memory to emerge. Once again, let yourself remember the details of that period or experience—the environment, sights, smells, voices, sounds. What people were around you?

Ask yourself: *who* had this experience? *Who* lived through adolescence or late childhood? *Who* am I? Experience this sense of *I-ness*.

Now recall a time of pain or crisis in your life. Any time, recent or long ago. Remember what that was like for you. See yourself living that experience, all the circumstances of it, who was involved, what it was about.

Now ask yourself: *who* experienced this crisis? *Who* lived through it? Again, as much as you are able to, sense this YOU, this *I* that did so.

Now recall a very special moment from your life, a time in which you felt very much in tune with yourself, a peak experience. Don't just mentally remember it, let yourself re-experience it in your imagination. What was the situation, who were you with and what were you doing? What were the good feelings you were having then, during this special moment?

Ask yourself: *who* had this special experience? *Who* am I? Let yourself experience this sense of *I-ness*, of being uniquely who you are.

Realize now that as a person who lives in the here and now, you also have a future. There will be a future for you. The future is not going to happen to someone else; it is *your* future. Place yourself in your future, in whichever way you want to imagine it. Even then this *thread* continues. *Who* has a future?

Now begin to sense that there is someone or a place in you that has provided this continuity, this *sameness*. You are the same you that you were as a baby, a child, an adolescent (and adult), in your crisis, in your special moment, and in your future. There exists the ONE in you who has not changed, although *all* these experiences have.

Focus your awareness towards this place that gives you a sense of identity, of me-ness, of *I-amness*. As you breathe in move deeper into that place and as you breathe out let yourself be filled with the sense of I-ness. (At least two minutes silence.)

Processing the experience:
Following this experience, let's discuss the idea of this thread of continuity and identity, of there being a part of us which remains the same throughout all our life and throughout all our experiences. What was that exercise like for you all? Who would like to share? What does this experience mean to you? How could it be useful to you to maintain this sense of identity in your life?

WATCHING OUR INNER PROCESSES
This dis-identification exercise is a meditation, which begins to foster the ability to observe one's inner processes as a means of gaining *psychological distance*. This distance provides a way of becoming self-aware and aids in creating a proper sense of proportion regarding the incessant flow of mental activity. It is the first essential step in expanding consciousness and in recognizing the Self which is beyond all mental activity.
Age: fourteen–adult
Time: 10 minutes for the exercise
      optional: 10 minutes for processing the experience
Exercise:
Sit comfortably and relax; as your body begins to quieten down, let your eyelids close. Relax in the darkness, allowing your body to become more peaceful and comfortable. Find a place in your body where you can feel your pulse and, when you do, rest your fingers lightly on it. Get in touch with the quiet rhythm of your pulse as it moves blood through your body.

Now in the quiet, begin *watching* the thoughts and feelings that come through your mind. Just look and listen for the pictures or sounds in your head. Pictures, voices, scenes, music, whatever comes. Just watch and listen. Just observe this flow of content. If you find yourself lost in thought, simply return to watching and listening (five to ten minutes).

Now in the future, when you find yourself angry, sad, bored, or in any kind of mood, you can watch and listen to what is going on inside your head. This will help you to get more in touch with what you are experiencing.

When you feel ready open your eyes.

Processing the experience: (Optional)
Would anyone like to share that experience? What is the value of this exercise? How could it be useful to you in your daily life?

BASIC SELF-IDENTIFICATION I
The exercise of *dis-identification* and *Self-identification* can facilitate the experience of *inner freedom* and the power to *choose* to be identified *with* or dis-identified *from* any aspect of our personality, according to what is most appropriate in any situation. We can learn to master, direct and utilize *all* the elements and aspects of our personality in an inclusive and harmonious way.

This exercise has the purpose of achieving consciousness of the Self, as well as promoting the ability to focus attention sequentially on the main personality aspects, feelings, thoughts, and sensations. In the form which follows, the first phase of the exercise, *dis-identification*, consists of three parts. It deals with the physical, emotional, and mental levels of awareness. Dis-identification leads to the Self-identification phase, the recognition of oneself as a pure centre of awareness and being.*

Age: fourteen–adult
Time: 20 minutes
Exercise:
Sit with your body in a comfortable position and slowly take a few deep breaths. Follow me as I make the following

---

*Adapted from an exercise by Roberto Assagioli in *The Act of Will* (Turnstone Press, 1984).

affirmation, slowly and thoughtfully:

1. I *have* a body, and I am more than my body. My body may find itself in different conditions of health and sickness, it may be rested or tired, but it is not my *self*, my real 'I'. I value my body, it is precious, and it is necessary if I am to experience and to act in the outer world. I treat it well, I keep it in good health, but it is not my true self. I *have* a body and I am more than my body.

2. I *have* emotions and I am more than my emotions. My emotions are constantly changing, sometimes in harmony, sometimes contradictory. They may swing from love to hostility, from calm to anger, from joy to sorrow, and yet my *essence*, my true nature, does not change. 'I' remain. Though a wave of anger may temporarily submerge me, I know that it will pass in time. Therefore I am not this anger, or any other temporary feeling. Since I can observe and understand my emotions, and then gradually learn to direct, utilize and integrate them, it is clear that they are not myself. I *have* emotions and I am more than my emotions.

3. I *have* a mind and I am more than my mind. My mind is a valuable tool of discovery and expression, but it is not the essence of my being. Its contents are constantly changing as it grasps new ideas, knowledge and experience. Sometimes my mind is clear and sometimes cloudy. Sometimes it refuses to obey me. Therefore it cannot be *me*, my *self*. It is what I use to gain knowledge in regard to both the inner and the outer worlds, but it is not my self. I *have* a mind and I am more than my mind.

4. What am I then? What remains after having dis-identified myself from my body, my feelings and my mind? It is the essence of myself, a centre of pure consciousness. It is the permanent factor in the ever-changing flow of my personal life. It is that which gives me a sense of being, of permanence, of inner balance. I affirm my identity with this centre and realize its permanency and its energy. I am a centre of being and of will, capable of observing, directing and using all my mental, emotional and physical processes. I am I.

BASIC SELF-IDENTIFICATION II

This exercise is an adaptation of basic Self-Identification I and uses a different language and tone.

Age: fourteen–adult

Time: 20 minutes
Exercise:
Sit in a comfortable position. Close your eyes, relax, and breathe deeply. Become aware of your body right now. Notice how your body is feeling. Notice what sensations pass through it right now. Be aware of how your body was different when you were younger, a different size and shape than it has now. It had different sensations, and it will change again as you grow older. Your body keeps changing from day to day: sometimes it is energetic and alert, sometimes tired and frail.

As you are aware of your body, ask yourself *who* is aware? Who is aware of this body that is constantly changing? *Who has a body?*

Now focus your attention on your feelings. Become aware of what you are feeling right now. Your feelings too are in a constant process of change. One moment they are joyful, then sad, then angry. They can move from joy to sadness, from love to hostility.

As you are aware of your feelings, ask yourself *who is aware? Who has feelings?*

Finally, become aware of your thoughts. With the same impartial attitude sit back and watch your thoughts pass through your mind. What are you thinking right now? Perhaps you have thoughts about what I'm saying, about this exercise. ... Your mind is generally in a constant state of change. Your thoughts are sometimes clear and direct; sometimes chaotic and confused. When you were young you believed many things that you don't believe now. In the future this will again happen. Your thoughts, attitudes and belief systems are constantly changing.

In the light of this, ask yourself: *who is aware? Who has a mind?*

Experience yourself as a point of consciousness beyond your body, your feelings, and your mind. A point of awareness and will. Recognize yourself as a being who has the wonderful resources of body, feelings, and mind. Think about the *one* in you who remains the same. Who you are is greater and beyond your personality.

Affirm your sense of pure beingness, of being a Self, a centre of 'I'-ness. Allow yourself to experience fully that 'I'. Experience your being. As you experience it imagine how long exactly a second is. A second of time. Sense how long a second of time is. What's that like? One second of time.

Then experience and imagine how long one minute is. How long is one minute? And if that's a minute, how long is one hour? Sense how long one hour is.

From there try to sense or imagine one day. Imagine twenty-four hours. If that's a day, how long is a week? Allow yourself to experience fully a week.

Now consider the span of one month in time.

And then one year. How long is ten years? Can you sense or feel how long ten years is?

How about one hundred years? What is that like?

Now consider one thousand years. How long is one thousand years? Allow yourself to experience that, the length of one thousand years.

And what about one million years? And how about one billion years? Can you allow yourself to sense one billion years?

And now, can you conceive eternity?

Staying connected with the experience of eternity, gradually begin to become aware of your body. Bring back with you the sense of eternity and your place in it, your sense of pure beingness, of pure I-amness, of being who you are—a Self.

Chapter 7

BEYOND WHAT WE THINK WE ARE

Our normal waking consciousness, rational consciousness as we call it, is but one special type of consciousness, whilst all about it, parted from it by the flimsiest of screens, there lies potential forms of consciousness entirely different. We may go through life without suspecting their existence, but apply the requisite stimulus, and at a touch they are there in all their completeness, definite types of mentality which probably somewhere have their field of adaptation and application. No account of the universe in its totality can be final which leaves these other forms of consciousness quite disregarded.

William James

The word spiritual does not refer to religious matters, so-called. All activity which drives the human being forward towards some form of development—physical, emotional, mental, intuitional, social—if it is in advance of his present state is essentially spiritual in nature and is indicative of the livingness of the inner Divine Entity. The spirit of man is undying; it forever endures, progressing from point to point and stage to stage upon the path of evolution, unfolding steadily and sequentially the Divine attributes and aspects.

Roberto Assagioli

So far we have explored the development of the personality of a young person and have addressed what is called their *personal psychosynthesis*. Personal psychosynthesis is a process which aims to build a personality which is free from emotional blocks, has a command over all its functions, and a clear awareness of its own centre. Transpersonal psychosynthesis is a process which enables the individual to explore those regions full of mystery and wonder beyond ordinary awareness, which we call the superconscious—the wellspring of higher intuitions, inspirations, ethical imperatives and states of illumination. This exploration culminates with the discovery of the Self, our true essence beyond all masks and conditioning.

This transpersonal dimension may well be the heart of the matter and the value of taking a deeper look at it is great. What precisely is its value and how can it serve us? What can we hope to gain by seeking to contact and experience this so-called *higher* or *deeper* level of our being? Paradoxically, the answer lies in the question—hope. Without the existence, or at least the potential, of a level of life which transcends our day-to-day living, the human condition might sometimes appear to be hopeless, complex and confusing. Without some kind of vision which reaches beyond existential reality, the task of realizing a fulfilling life would be overwhelming. Contact with this mysterious dimension also promises to enhance development of the physical, emotional, and mental functions leading to the formation of identity. Metaphorically speaking, the proper soil can be prepared and made fertile for the future blossoming flower.

It is only through an awakening of the transpersonal dimension that the answers to many of the most profound existential questions of adolescence may be found. It is this dimension that builds a bridge between the everyday functioning of the personality and the deeper Self of which most of us are dimly aware. A fundamental assumption of psychosynthesis is that each individual has within himself potentially *all* that he needs in order to grow and develop. Whether this assumption is true or not I leave to speculation. What we can take as *truth* is that to work psychospiritually within a positive and affirming framework yields more effective and healthy results. The main purpose of working with adolescents in the transpersonal domain is to give them a sense of who they are, where they wish to go with their life, and to develop the necessary strengths and qualities to enable them to move in their chosen direction. It includes a search for meaning, value and purpose, for harmony and balance within the personality, and for a deeper more authentic Self.

At an early age some children show an interest in philosophy, and in moral and spiritual subjects. Sometimes children are interested in issues like the origin and destiny of man, and the meaning of life, and may ask for explanations of the process of life and death, of time and space. Children, from time to time, experience deep intuitions and spiritual illuminations. A child's curiosity and wonder about life as he experiences something for the first time, or surprises himself with an action never performed before, are examples of this.

A cross-cultural research project is currently being undertaken in psychosynthesis to explore children's perspectives on fundamental philosophical issues. Children from three to ten years old are being interviewed in many countries. Questions that have successfully elicited meaningful responses from children cover a wide range of areas including: the origin of life and the world, the origins of self, pre-natal and post-mortem states of being, the genesis of self-consciousness, the purpose of life, the structure of the universe and the process of development. The study so far has indicated that children do not simply parrot the answers of adults but often formulate original and creative concepts that are clearly not learned responses. Some recurrent underlying patterns have emerged indicating an awareness of an essential unity of mankind and oneness of all life. Common themes are: oneness, bliss, non-separation, fusion of opposites, mythical figures and other ways in which the transpersonal realm has been described by philosophy and mythology of all ages.[1] Children seem to have a deep knowing, albeit abstract and symbolic, of a fundamental alrightness in the universe.

I believe that *all* children naturally possess the potential for spiritual experience and insight, which unfortunately tends to be culturally conditioned out of them. For example, since 1960 a substantial amount of research has been done on altruism, some of which focused on altruism in infants and children. It was found that infants and children do inherently possess and demonstrate altruistic tendencies. How the environment responds to these tendencies determines their further elaboration or death. *We* are the environment, you and I. If spontaneous altruism is responded to favourably, the behaviour is reinforced; whereas if the adult world does not notice and affirm the behaviour, it will eventually disappear.

Children, of any age, have a right to receive adequate answers, which will satisfy their cravings and encourage the recognition of spiritual areas. Dr Assagioli wrote:

> Their questions must be taken seriously; one can use such opportunities to instill in them a spiritual conception of life, allow them to feel the greatness and beauty of the universe and the admirable order that characterises it . . . at the same time one must observe and encourage all spontaneous manifestations of a spiritual nature such as higher aspirations, intuitions and illuminations that might arise in them.[2]

Gerald Weinstein, an educator from the University of Massachusetts, supports this statement when he says, 'Teaching should be orientated towards long term internalisation rather than short term arousal. The concept of humanistic education should focus more on teaching the irreversible, increasing adequate structures of intelligent living.'[3]

Spontaneous spiritual experiences occur in children and adolescents more frequently than we might realize. Their consciousness is more open than that of adults to *all* impressions, which includes those from the transpersonal dimension. These experiences are usually fleeting and easily lost under the strong impact of the incessant stream of other input upon their consciousness. We can be on the lookout for signs of these experiences, encourage their recognition and appreciate their value.

How can we know when a child or an adolescent is having a transpersonal experience or attempting to share a previous one? What is the quality and discernable nature of transpersonal experiences? They come in many forms and vary in intensity and length. There is no recipe or set form. The best insurance is to be somewhat familiar with these states ourselves. In my work I have never found an adult who has not had some kind of superconscious experience; although we may not define such experiences as spiritual. I highly recommend that the educator first participate in the transpersonal exercises himself, so that these states are familiar and resonate with shared experiences from the young.

However, there are some universally characteristic forms

that transpersonal experiences are reported to take. They are:

— an insight;
— the sudden solution of a difficult problem;
— seeing one's life in perspective and having a clear sense of purpose;
— a transfigured vision of external reality;
— the apprehension of some truth concerning the nature of the universe;
— a sense of unity with all beings and of sharing everyone's destiny;
— illumination;
— an extraordinary inner silence;
— waves of luminous joy;
— liberation;
— cosmic humour;
— a deep sense of gratefulness;
— an exhilarating sense of dance;
— resonating with the essence of beings and things that we come in contact with;
— loving all persons in one person;
— feeling oneself to be a channel for a wider, stronger force to flow through;
— ecstasy;
— an intimation of profound mystery and wonder;
— the delight of beauty;
— creative inspiration;
— a sense of boundless compassion;
— transcendence of time and space as we know them.[4]

Our language is inadequate for an appropriate description of such experiences and young people in particular may have difficulty recounting them. The rhythm of transpersonal experiences can vary greatly, sometimes exploding with intensity and brightness, while at other times taking the form of a more gradual realization. When adults disregard, dismiss, or ridicule such experiences, the natural reaction of a child or adolescent is to repress them and learn to deny their reality. This may result in a future inhibition of transpersonal consciousness. I have often heard adults dismiss their past magic moments as *youthful idealism*, the product of not having one's feet on the ground. These experiences are even rationalized away as 'regressive tendencies' and as an avoidance of reality. How tragic it is that in these ways we slowly kill contact with our own essential beingness and, worse still, with that of our children.

There are five general principles to follow which encourage such transpersonal awareness in a child or adolescent. They are:

1. The importance of cultivating in young people a sense of beauty, chiefly the appreciation of the natural environment in its varied and diverse forms.
2. Cultivating a sense of wonder, admiration and reverence for all life and life forms.
3. Presenting the young with human examples as role models of the spiritual life in its many aspects: great religious figures, the heroes who attained great heights of human achievement, not as warriors or conquerors but as humanitarians, artists, and scientists, past and present. Reading and sharing the autobiographies or biographies of these great people is a good way of doing this.
4. Placing due interest and importance on the inner, vital, spiritual aspects of life, form and symbols. This will be covered in the transpersonal exercise section.
5. Wisely adapting other methods of promoting spiritual awakening and understanding for the use of young people, including the use of meditation in the classroom.[5]

The Transpersonal Dimension and Its Workings
At some point during middle to late adolescence, most young people begin to regulate the functioning of their personality to various degrees, and begin to isolate their personal identity. They may also begin to sense the existence of, and the need for, something which is beyond their everyday self. This may be overtly and disarmingly conscious, or it may be apparently dormant and quietly working beneath conscious awareness. For example, the adolescent may become increasingly interested in the meaning and possibilities of life. He may be having experiences which fill him with new strong and joyful feelings, or he may become aware of the confusion and pain in the larger world. These experiences are not necessarily only

positive. As he grows out of childhood naïvety and trust in the benevolence of the adult world, he may question things he thought he knew. He may realize more and more that the answers he had been given no longer ring true for him.

In some adolescents, however, the transpersonal may seem to be dormant, because on the surface not much appears to be happening. An adolescent's psyche will only allow into consciousness that which is appropriate for him. We may be disappointed if we expect to see immediate results from our guidance and input. It is helpful to realize that the thrust that an educator gives will lie like a seed in the earth, and we should not expect it to bear fruit in one season.

More often, however, the transpersonal may manifest in clear and communicable forms, especially among those adolescents with a fairly well rounded personality, and those whose experiences were not previously negated. Here, our task is to work with what already is in their consciousness and to help them to understand the meaning and value of transpersonal experiences. Value is obtained when the young person knows how these experiences can be grounded and integrated into his daily life. Given that the adolescent's personality may not yet be capable of effectively expressing these energies, this grounding often needs attention and work. Sometimes it is necessary to eliminate the obstacle, such as a lack of self-confidence, fear or anger, to the full expression of his transpersonal qualities. Appropriate grounding techniques are provided in the transpersonal exercise section.

Superconscious energies are particularly active in certain young people, who seem to have more sensitivity and vulnerability to the forces of their psyche. This sensitivity may be both a gift and a detriment. Such young people may be prone to the existential crisis, or the crisis of duality, suffer from excessive overstimulation, or be so blocked psycho-logically that they become overwhelmed by superconscious experiences. After all, superconscious experiences manifest through our personality and, depending upon psychological health, can be received, absorbed and utilized, or rejected, distorted and misused. Again we see the importance of actively working towards the full development of all personality functions. This work will provide the foundation upon which to build the transpersonal. Transpersonal energy is the life-force of Self-realization but its power demands a solid psychological base.

Self-discovery

We all know that consciousness of the personal self disappears during sleep, under hypnosis and anaesthesia, and reappears upon awakening. However, this personal self is just a reflection of some centre in a field of consciousness, which is much deeper and which we may call the Self.[6] Through fostering expansion of personal consciousness, we increasingly open up to and begin to experience the transpersonal dimension. It is a natural evolutionary progression for this to occur. This movement from personal to transpersonal awareness expresses itself as a movement from concern with the practical business of living and self-aggrandizement towards a need for fulfilment and a recognition of a deeper meaning in life.

Without acceptance of the existence of this deeper Self, it is difficult to explain satisfactorily the duration of the sense of consciousness, or the feeling of consistent personal identity, through changing states of mind. The fact that we ordinarily have no consciousness of this Self is not surprising, since our awareness is occupied with the continual flow of varied and diverse psychophysical states. Yet from time to time many people have a longing for some ineffable depth, or an unquestionable knowing that this depth exists, which Assagioli described as *divine homesickness*. To others it is just a theory but it makes sense, to the point of beckoning them to explore more. For others still, there has never been an awareness of anything beyond everyday existence, but some life-experience, often of an earth-shattering nature, like the death of a loved one, when least expected pushes through a revelation of a mysterious world.

It is difficult to define the Self. The transcendent nature of it is so far beyond our normal range of experience that it also tends to be beyond our power of imagination. We form our concept of what the Self is like on the basis of superconscious experiences, thereby easily confusing the two. Some clarification between the Self and the superconscious is necessary. Transpersonal experiences which *occur* in the superconscious tend to be mystical, aesthetic, intuitive, and illuminating.

Assagioli said that they are: 'processes, living processes. They belong to the world of becoming and even at the transpersonal level there is this wonderful process of becoming, of growth, of all phases of the superconscious. But the Self in contra-distinction is stable, firm, permanent, or to use the philo-sophical word, "ontological". It is pure being.'[7]

All of our transpersonal experiences are further elabora-tions of the emanations, qualities, and energies of the Self; but not the Self itself. We may use the analogy of the sun to illustrate this point. The Self is like the sun, which is at the distant centre of our solar system and remains there, yet its rays and energies pervade the entire solar system. Likewise, the radiance and emanations of the Self pervade our entire being.

It is nearly impossible to describe adequately the experi-ence of the Self. In the East, it has been described variously as: the void, the point of no-*thingness*, Tao (in its transcendent sense), pure beingness, essential energy, the jewel in the lotus. It is not an *experience*; it is the source of all experience (as the sun is to us the source of all light). The *knowing* of our Self has within it superconscious qualities of perfect peace, stillness, unity and serenity, which all point to a transcendent reality. There is a blending of individuality and universality, of feeling both unique *and* a part of something greater, a solidarity with all life. A paradox exists between becoming and being; that of increasingly evolving towards something that is bigger than we presently are, yet already knowing and being *fully* who we are. The Self is more simply described as a centre of authenticity, of inner goodness or wholeness, of essence.

Superconscious is the term used to designate the higher (or sometimes experienced as deeper depending upon one's inner cosmology) spiritual region of the psyche. The differ-ence between the superconscious and the personality is one of *level*, rather than of *nature*. Superconscious experiences fundamentally consist of an emerging awareness of the activity occurring in the higher levels of human awareness.[8] They carry with them a *qualitative* charge and transcend our normally limited consciousness. They bring a sense of timelessness, of formlessness, providing a rare and precious glimpse of a reality not fully *known* to us.

We might see the Self as radiating a magnetic field around it, which we call the superconscious. At any time in our daily living we may have brief experience of the energies or archetypal qualities contained within the superconscious. By archetypal I mean 'a universal principle which unifies, heals and gives meaning'. In these moments we feel closest to ourselves, or more deeply in touch with who we really are. An example of this would be the especially vivid and inspiring moments that Abraham Maslow referred to as *peak experiences,* a generalization for the best moments of being a human, the deepest and happiest moments of life, the experiences of greatest joy. These peak experiences can happen during or through any moment of living: through contact with nature, an experience of beauty, close contact with a loved one, the birth of a child, a simple moment of recognizing the symbolic meaning of an everyday activity; or sometimes through more negative moments of trauma—the loss of a job, the death of a loved one, a failure of some sort, an accident. Its sources are many and varied.

Maslow takes this idea one step further, to say that these peak experiences are indeed universal to human beings, and in his research he found that the experiences were frequently described with the same words: truth, beauty, wholeness, aliveness, uniqueness, perfection, completion, justice, order, simplicity, richness, effortlessness, playfulness and self-sufficiency. He also believed there to be 'meta-needs' (needs for beauty, truth, justice, etc.), which were as basic to us as our biological needs, the frustration of which would produce neurosis as surely as the frustration of our biological needs produces pathology. For those who experience these precious moments, they are subjectively felt as a step forward in personal evolution and they have enormous value which persists through time and influences the way that people conduct their lives. They symbolize a revolution of what was previously only in a potential state.

A working hypothesis is that the Self is at the core of the superconscious, just as the 'I' or personal self is at the core of the personality and its various functions (physical, emotional and mental). Interaction between the Self and the 'I' can occur or flow in either direction. When the contents of the superconscious descend into our conscious experience, we receive inspiration, intuition, insight or peak experiences. These moments *happen* to us, particularly when we least expect them or have not been actively seeking them. However, the *flow* may also occur in the other direction, through elevating our personality, through consciously aspiring, in a realistic, grounded and purposeful way, towards the heights or depths of our being. It is through this conscious and purposeful exploration that many of the deeper difficulties and crises of adolescence can be addressed and some positive progress made. Working with the transpersonal dimension, for example by the use of the exercises provided in this book, can help the adolescent to find answers to perplexing and painful crises, and to work actively to discover his own nature, his deep wishes, what he seeks and yearns for, what really satisfies him, what his values are and his temperament and constitution.

Self-guidance

Another facet to the Self is its service to us as a guiding and directing force. Based on a principle I have discussed earlier, that the individual has within him everything he needs to grow and develop, including the *answers* to his personal questions, we might say that we each possess a source of inner wisdom. This source contains within it truth lying hidden and often forgotten. Our scientific culture, which demands objective proof, denies our subjective experience and brings about this forgetfulness. The Self is constantly pointing the way for us should we just pay attention. It knows more essentially who we are and may even have a plan or path that is ideal for us, as in the Eastern concept of *dharma*. We can symbolically contact this *inner guide* through the use of guided imagery. For example in *psychological mountain climbing*, we imagine that we meet a wise and loving person on top of a mountain, who knows all about us, loves us unconditionally and possesses the ability both to guide and to heal us. He or she is not caught up in the struggles of everyday life but carries a vision of life and our place in it. He or she represents the inner *knowing* that we all have but only occasionally experience spontaneously. This *symbol of wisdom* is a way of contacting this inner expertise, which can truly be trusted. It functions as a symbol of the Self and opens us up to a deeper awareness of our selves.

The idea of a source of inner wisdom, love and guidance may initially be received by an adolescent with some discomfort. He may have a resistance to appearing too soft, loving, or sentimental. His surface response might be one of embarrassment; but once this initial discomfort passes, the inner guide may become consistently available. It is a sense of *knowing* or *rightness*, or inner *authority*, that a young person is fundamentally seeking to find within himself, whether he is conscious of it or not. The more an adolescent is in contact with this knowing, the less dependent he is upon environmental support. This greatly aids the establishment of his identity and autonomy.

This is nothing new. It is conventionally understood to be the development of intuitive faculties. The technique of seeking inner guidance can be used on any occasion but it is particularly helpful at certain moments in life like: when seeking the answer to a personal problem; when needing to experience more self-love and acceptance; when resolving conflicts with self or others; when facing an important choice; when feeling misunderstood and alone; or when searching for the answers to existential questions, such as the meaning of life. It is not limited to personal use but can give insight into complex moral or social issues.

Of course the answers received from such explorations should not be taken as gospel truths but, rather, as working hypotheses. Discrimination is an important quality for every human being to develop and the authenticity of inner guidance must always be verified. How? By examining the answer received in the light of known rational criteria. The ultimate test is in the *living* of these answers and through this process we gradually learn what is true intuition and what is coloured by various psychological distortions. The symbology of the superconscious requires interpretation as if reading poetry. Thus the intuition often provides abstract answers which need bringing down into the practical world.

Transpersonal Will

There are some older children, but more often those in late adolescence, who experience the emergence of the transpersonal will—a psychodynamic thrust towards what one is meant to do and be. This builds upon previously mentioned qualities of the personal will. Becoming what we are meant to be, or discovering a fundamental task in life, is an experience that can occur which gives meaning and value to life. If this thrust is respected and honoured we will find psychological health and well-being; thwarting it may lead us toward neurosis.

This thrust is not just an idea or concept—it has a force or power of its own, an energetic impulse and sense of rightness; but it can easily be betrayed, forgotten or repressed. It could be seen as a dynamic plan which is trying to realize itself in the individual's life. We could call this force the transpersonal will, or the will of the Self, because it is above the ordinary interplay of day-to-day wants and desires. It is something much more profound. It could be extremely useful to call upon the transpersonal will during career planning or before choosing educational focus for one's future.

In Other Words

The Self cannot take part in any activity. It is not the actor of our parts, the thinker of our thoughts, the feeler of our feelings. This role is taken on by its reflection or representative, the personal 'I', and once the existence of the Self is recognized, an individual knows that who he is is essentially beyond all words or action. The transpersonal Self does not have to be perceived by a bounded self; but it gradually reveals itself to us. A *sense of being emerges* which pervades our awareness.

Our identification with the realm of the personality is what blocks us from its realization. Dis-identification works by a process of gently slowing down the activity of the personality and by emptying its contents until it reaches what T. S. Eliot poetically described as a 'still point of a turning world'. At this point where there is no action, and hence no actor, the true Self stands revealed. Naturally such glimpses of the Self do not amount to full self-realization; but through regular practice of this technique an individual becomes increasingly acquainted with deeper levels of himself and begins to integrate this into his active life.

Another important aspect of the process of self-realization is that it enhances the way in which we experience and relate to other human beings. Our habit is to view people and other elements of life only superficially and to perceive them as separate from us, and somehow different. We experience ourselves as fundamentally isolated from others;

but contact with the transpersonal dimension is consistently reported to bring a sense of solidarity with all beings, and of being an essential part of a larger whole. Dr Assagioli wrote: 'A spiritual conception of life is an immense help. Such a conception enables us to look upon our fellow human beings not as separate bodies or personalities, which are an end in themselves but as spiritual Beings, pilgrims on the path of manifestation.'[9] Martin Buber would describe this as an 'I/Thou' attitude, which I will go into further in Chapter 8.

With transpersonal development, it is seen that individual interest is not to be set against the interest of others. The individual is not forced to act in an unselfish way, but he comes to see that he is not an isolated entity. He cannot *win* against his environment, nor is any battle ultimately necessary. The nature of our educational system gives ample opportunity to bring this reality to a young person's attention and can evoke the necessary consciousness for appropriate behaviour.

EXERCISES

WHERE AM I GOING AND WHAT'S IN MY WAY?
This free drawing exercise provides the participant with an assessment and look at the whole of his life. In a symbolic way, it explores where the individual comes from, where he is going, what is blocking him and what he needs to develop and nurture within himself. It facilitates the discovery of the existence of *meaning* and a sense of purpose to life. It can be used as a preparatory session for beginning Transpersonal work.

Age: fourteen–adult
Time: 45 minutes for the exercise
   45 minutes for processing the experience
Equipment: Five sheets of drawing paper and crayons for each participant.
Exercise:
Sit comfortably, take a few minutes to relax, and find a quiet place inside. I will be giving you some topics for reflection and you will make a drawing of your experience.

Let's begin by thinking about change. What does change

mean to you? Just reflect on the concept of change. How do you perceive change? Allow an image to emerge that is symbolic of what change means to you. Try not to censor or judge your images. Allow the image to become vivid and clear. See what the message of this image is. Perceive what it communicates to you. When you are ready, open your eyes and draw your sense of the experience of change.

Where do you come from? Think about how far you have come in your life so far. You have grown and changed a lot over the years. Think about your life's journey, the joys, the pains, the highs, the lows. Think how you are different now from how you used to be. Sense how your life has unfolded. Now allow a symbol to appear that represents where you come from. Again accept whatever image comes, and allow it to become vivid and clear. Spend a moment with this image. What does it tell you? How do you feel? When you are ready, open your eyes and draw your sense of this image.

Where are you going in your life? What is the dearest and most creative possibility for you? What is most meaningful and important? What is the direction that you deeply wish to go in? Now, allow an image or a symbol to appear that represents all this. As before, spend some time with this image. Learn its message and feel its meaning for you. When you feel ready, open your eyes and draw your experience of where you are going.

What's in your way? What is blocking you from going where you want to go? What is the major difficulty that stops you? Allow an image to appear that is symbolic of or related to this obstacle which is stopping you from going where you really want to go. Allow it to become vivid and clear. Spend a moment with the image. When you feel ready, open your eyes and draw your sense of this.

What do you need to develop and nurture in yourself in order to go through your obstacle and to go where you really want to go with your life? What is it that you need to nourish inside you? What quality do you need to foster in yourself? Again, let an image or a symbol come for this. Take a good look at it. What does it mean to you? When you are ready, open your eyes and draw your sense or feeling of this image.

Processing the experience:
Find a partner and share your five drawings. Help each other to define clearly what is blocking you and what you need to develop or nurture in yourself. How can you do that? What steps can you take?

AFFIRMING THE RICHNESS AND THE DEPTH OF WHO WE ARE

As adolescents increasingly begin to *know* their personal identity, they can come to the recognition that it is not their ultimate Self. This recognition can be both inspiring and liberating, bringing with it the experience of the vastness of each individual's potential. Life can contain the *promise* of something richer and more expanded than we normally allow ourselves to perceive. This exercise is designed to facilitate this recognition and provide the experience of a deeper, inner essence.

Age: sixteen–adult
Time: 30 minutes for the exercise
       20 minutes for processing the experience
Equipment: Psychological workbook.
Exercise:
Have your writing materials nearby. Inhale and ask yourself: WHO AM I? and allow an answer to this question to come. Write down the answer when you feel like it, but ask the question each time, don't just write about who you are.

Try to go as deep into yourself as you can, towards the core of your being. Start at the most immediate level, moving towards the deepest sense of who you are. You can shift levels from depth to more surface, but gradually move towards your core. (Five minutes.)

Now share with a partner what you have found so far. As you share, make it clear what you see as the most central core of you and what is periphery and more superficial. (Ten minutes.)

Close your eyes again and go back inside. Breathe deeply for a moment.

This Self that you are is a deep sense of being, of unlimited potential. You may have experienced your Self in a special moment of your life. Recall now some special experiences of this type, when you felt really close to your *Self.*

It may have been with nature, or music, or with another person. Recreate that experience in your imagination right now. Don't just think about it, but relive it. What was it like for you? What was the quality of that experience? Find a word or words that best describe the quality of that special moment for you.

Now I would like you to remember something different. Recall a time from your life when you experienced a *sense of rightness*. A time when you had a real *knowing* that something was *right* for you. This is not a rightness that comes from outside you, or from the environment, but a rightness that comes from *inside* you. What was it like knowing that something was right for you? What is rightness? What was the quality of this experience for you? Again see if you can find a word or words that best describe the quality of this experience of rightness.

Now switch senses once more, and think of three people that you admire and respect. These people can be living or dead, and you may know them personally or not. Who are some people that you really admire and respect? As you think of these people, tune into the quality in them that you admire or respect. What's the quality in that person?

As you tune into the quality that you admire and respect in these people, see if you are willing to *own* those qualities as something that *you* too have. Some say that you can't be aware of something in someone else, unless you have it too, at least potentially so. Right now, see if you're willing to re-own these positive projections.

Now keeping in mind the quality of your peak experience, the quality of your experience of rightness, and some positive projections: experience that all of this is *inside* you, is an essential part of who you really are. These experiences are a part of your Self that has value and meaning and knows what is right. See if you are willing to express those qualities, to live them in your daily life. . . .

When you feel ready, slowly bring yourself back to this room and take a few minutes to write about your experiences.

Processing the experience:
With the same partner with whom you shared earlier, talk about this part of the exercise. Help each other to define the

qualities of the three experiences, and look at how those
qualities are inside you right now. Look also at *how* and *if*
those qualities are being expressed in your life. If not, look at
what it is in *you* that blocks you from expressing them more.

THE INNER DIALOGUE

Each of us has a source of understanding and wisdom within,
which knows who we are, where we have been, and perhaps
where we are going. It is in tune with our unfolding purpose
and it senses clearly the next steps to be taken to fulfil this
purpose. As we contact it, we can better recognize the
difficulties we are having in our growth and, with its help, we
can guide our awareness and will toward their resolution.
Rightly used, our inner guide can help us direct our energies
toward achieving increasing integration in our daily living,
and toward unifying into one reality the personal and
transpersonal dimensions of our lives.

Many images are associated with this source of inner
guidance. Common ones are the sun, a diamond, a fountain, a
star or point of light, an angel, an eagle, dove, or phoenix, the
Christ or the Buddha. Different images emerge to meet
different needs. The one most commonly associated with this
source is that of a wise and loving old man or woman.

These are two distinct archetypal images, with many
similarities but also specific differences. It is worthwhile
experimenting with both so as to know each well, and to know
when to use one or the other according to the specific needs of
the situation. In general, the wise old man is encouraging,
stimulating, inspiring; the wise old woman is more nurturing,
supportive, allowing. Over time the contact with this inner
source can grow, so that its love and wisdom increasingly can
guide our daily lives.

In the use of this exercise, two further mental processes
are necessary: *discrimination* and *interpretation*. We must learn
to discriminate between those images which carry true
wisdom and those which do not. For example, occasionally a
critical and authoritarian figure appears, one who is not truly
loving toward you. It can be the projection of a subpersonality
or a known person onto the superconscious, and discrimination must be used to recognize it for what it is and 'unmask' it.
Also, a positive projection onto the superconscious may result

in hearing what you want to, and not what is really being communicated.

Secondly, the message received is not always clear in its application and so must be interpreted correctly. A famous example of this is God's injunction to St Francis to 'Go and rebuild my church'. At first Francis thought this meant to rebuild the little ruined church of San Damiano outside the walls of Assisi, and only later did he realize its true import—to rebuild the whole Catholic Church!

Finally, though this contact is important, it is also important not to over-use it. The best procedure is first to explore as fully as possible the dimensions of the problem you are dealing with and then, if you find no solution, you can ask for guidance.*

Age: eight–adult

Time: 20 minutes for the exercise

20 minutes for processing the experience

Exercise:

After a few moments of physical relaxation, make an act of presence with yourself. You are aware, you are here, and ready to begin this journey.

You are in a valley, it's morning, a summer morning in a green valley. You can see green and flowers all around. Green, flowers, trees.

You see the mountain not very far from you and you start walking towards it. You enter a forest and feel its cleansing atmosphere, and you continue to walk in this forest, with its fresh atmosphere.

Then keep climbing on this gentle path that is going up. It is climbing and going higher and higher. Little by little you see the light and are getting out of the forest. You are really climbing now. There are rocks, beautiful granite rocks. You have the feeling of going up and up and upwards. It even requires some physical strain, and you have great strength to climb. If you need to you can use your hands to climb and you feel the smoothness of the rocks.

Now you are entering a cloud, and you see mist around you, and feel your own hands on the rocks. But keep climbing, slowly and persistently. You have a feeling of going up, of

*Unpublished article, Psychosynthesis Institute, San Francisco, California.

elevation, through the clouds, until finally the cloud dissolves and you get through it. You see again the sky, which is now deep blue and very clear. The air is pure and you breathe it and feel refreshed and energized.

You can keep climbing and going towards the top of the mountain. It is very easy to climb now and you are almost to the top. When you reach the top, stop for a moment, look around and see all the other mountains in the distance, the valley, some clouds; you are at a great height.

Now begin to feel the presence of a humorous, very wise, very loving person who is there for you. This being loves you very much. Get closer to him/her and feel the presence of wisdom and love. Look in the eyes of this person, and begin to talk with him/her. Say whatever you want to say, ask whatever you want to ask. You can seek guidance on problems, questions, anything you wish. Take some time to talk with this wise and loving being.

Then—listen for the answers. These answers may come with or without words. Any answer might come; listen in silence. I'll give you a few minutes of silence to be receptive.

Whether the answer came or not, slowly come back to this room. Take your time, there is no hurry. When you are back, take a few minutes to record this experience in your psychological workbook.

Processing the experience:
Break into small groups of two to four people and each have some time to share your experience. Remember that some-times the answers come to us at a later time.

Talk about the meaning of this experience for you. If you received inner guidance, what does it mean in terms of your everyday life? How can you apply this experience to your life?

EXERCISE OF INTEGRATING TRANSPERSONAL EXPERIENCES

A common experience for all of us is a deep longing and desire to live life as fully and meaningfully as possible. We all have a sense of our potential and indeed sometimes experience that potential. When our experience of who we really are is *actualized* in our everyday life, there is a sense of fulfilment and meaning. When our daily life is *not* a reflection of this deeper self, we experience frustration, disillusionment and pain. We can learn to integrate consciously our experiences of our true self with our everyday existence through this exercise, so that they are bridged with our present reality.

This exercise provides a *model* which can be used for deepening and integrating any transpersonal experience. It also demonstrates the importance and usefulness of bringing the transpersonal dimension and the personal dimension together.*

Age: sixteen–adult
Time: 45 minutes for the exercise
45 minutes for processing the experience
Equipment: Psychological workbook.
Exercise:
Close your eyes, relax, and find a quiet place inside. Recall an experience from the past (recently or long ago) when you had a real sense of who you really are. Recall an experience when you felt most fully yourself, most real and most alive. It can be any kind of experience. It may have been with nature, when you were alone, or with another person.

Go back to that experience in your imagination right now and relive it. Imagine that you are having it right now; visualize it as vividly and with as much detail as possible. Let it come alive. See where you were in this experience, what you were doing, and who you were with.

How were you feeling during this experience? What was happening in your body? What kinds of thoughts were you thinking? Be there now as much as you can, reliving this special moment or moments.

Now continue your recollections. Focus on what happened in the hours and days after it. What meaning did the experience have for you? What understanding and insights did it bring? How did you feel about it afterwards? Was there anyone with whom you tried to share it? If so, did they understand? In the days following it, did it cause any changes in your life?

Come back to the present with your awareness and take some time to write about this experience and the period

*This exercise was adapted from *Synthesis Journal,* Psychosynthesis Institute, San Francisco, California.

following it.

Close your eyes and go back to your inner world. Focus again on this experience you had and on the most meaningful aspects of it. Get in touch with its central quality. Try to summarize it with a word, phrase or symbol.

Now return with your imagination to the present. Take some time, visualizing yourself standing on top of a mountain on a clear sunny day. Look up and see the sun shining overhead, in a warm and beneficent way. Now imagine a ray of sunlight coming from the sun and shining on the ground next to you. Now you can see in the sun a very wise, old and loving person, whose eyes express great love for you. Gently and slowly this wise old being comes down from the sun on the ray of light and is soon standing next to you on the mountain top.

Tell the wise old being about your experience and its meaning. Find out what he or she has to tell you about it. Then ask this being how you can make this experience a part of your life now. Listen for suggestions and ask for clarification if necessary. This communication between you and the wise being may happen with or without words.

Now in your imagination turn towards your present life. See yourself expressing the *quality* of that experience in your life as it is now, or the understanding which comes from this experience in certain circumstances. Simply watch this happening. How could you be expressing this quality, or the meaning of this experience, in your life right now? Try to get a feeling of how that could happen.

When you feel ready, open your eyes and write about your experience of the wise being and of how you could be expressing the essence of this experience in your life right now.

While you are writing, look at your present life, the activities you are involved in, the relationships you have, and your plans for the future, to see where you would like to begin expressing the quality of your experience and the understanding that came from it. Ask yourself *how* you want to do this and *when*.

Processing the experience:
Find a partner to share this entire experience with. Your partner can help you to become more clear in any of the stages if you need to. Go step-by-step through the exercise in your

sharing, looking at what you need to do in order to bring this awareness more into your life.

IDEAL QUALITY MEDITATION

To have the ability to cultivate and nurture chosen psychological or transpersonal qualities is a skill for life. There are some qualities that feel most important at certain moments, new qualities seeking to emerge, or qualities needed in a particular circumstance of our life. This exercise serves as a model for the cultivation of any quality one may want to choose. It can be used, for example, to evoke courage in fearful situations, love in interpersonal relationships, strength in times of difficulty.

Age: eight–adult
Time: 15 minutes for the exercise
      15 minutes for processing the experience
Equipment: Psychological workbook.
Exercise:

Put your body in a comfortable position. Allow yourself to relax and breathe deeply.

Choose a quality that you would like to develop within yourself, to experience more in your life, and become more familiar with. Now imagine yourself as already having that quality. Have a visual image of yourself with it. What would you be like? What would you look like? Imagine that. See yourself expressing and having this quality already within you.

Imagine what your face would look like, your eyes, the expression you would have on your face. What would your body be like? What posture would it have? See yourself clearly as already having that quality. See an image of yourself before you.

Now step into this image. Become it, identify with it. You can put the image on as if it were a shirt or a dress. Feel what it is like now to have that quality already fully living within you. How do all parts of you feel? How does your body feel? Your emotions? Your mind?

Now imagine yourself to be in some everyday situation in which you can use and express this quality. It might be a situation where you really need this quality. You can even communicate it to others by your way of being. See yourself there now, living a real life situation with this quality available to you, as vividly and with as much detail as possible.

When you feel complete, quietly come back and take a few minutes to write about this experience.

Processing the experience:
Break into small groups and share your experience.

THE ROSE EXPERIENCE

This experience is symbolically associated with human experiences of evolution and development. It implies the passage from the potential to the actual, and it is unusually effective in stimulating and promoting the *opening* or *blossoming* of transpersonal consciousness. It also tends to instil within the participants an awareness of each other, a sense of brotherhood and the oneness of humanity.*

Age: fourteen–adult
Time: 20 minutes for the exercise
Equipment: Psychological workbook.
Exercise:
Sit comfortably, relax, and quiet yourself. Imagine that you are in a garden. It is the most incredible garden you have ever been in. It is extremely beautiful there. You are alone there in the garden, surrounded by nature. Spend a few moments *being* in this garden. Notice what the environment is like, enjoy the beauty surrounding you. Walk around visiting this garden. Feel the colours of the flowers, smell their fragrance.

You keep walking through the garden until you come to the centre of it, and there you see a rose bush with one unopened rosebud on top. You sit down beside this rose bush and look at the rosebud. As you watch now, the bud begins to open, it slowly begins to bloom.

You watch the bud slowly, slowly opening. As you watch, you suddenly realize that *you are* this unopened bud and *you are* starting to blossom. First your sepals begin to spread out and your bud itself is revealed. Now a tip of colour can be seen. Slowly your sepals separate little by little, curling their points outwards and downwards, revealing a perfectly shaped rosebud. Slowly this process of life is happening within you. Now your petals slowly begin to separate and to open. You are unfolding. This unfoldment has been natural and inevitable for you.

*This exercise was adapted from Robert Assagioli, *Psychosynthesis* (Turnstone Press, 1975).

You can feel and smell your intense fragrance with this opening, a delicate, pleasant scent. See your perfume wafting through the air, mingling with the scent of other roses and flowers. Now you become aware of other rose bushes near you. Let your perfume mingle with theirs. Notice how your roots come into contact with their roots. You share the same nutrients, the same water, the same sunshine. You feel in touch, in tune with the other roses. You feel one with them. Stay with this feeling of oneness, of inner calm, of peace, of radiance, for a few minutes.

Now become aware of where you are sitting, this room, this group, and slowly come back to the present. When you are ready, take a moment to write about your experience. Stay with your experience as you write.

THE TEMPLE OF SILENCE

Amidst the rush and noise of everyday life, to have the ability to create inner silence can be a welcome skill. Silence has often been used as a metaphor for the Self, for the pure being that is our core or essence. There is a place in each of us that is still and silent and is beyond the incessant stream of consciousness. To have the capacity to contact this place of stillness can be psychologically nourishing and regenerating. This guided visualization creates the experience of pure silence.*

Age: fourteen–adult
Time: 20 minutes
Equipment: Psychological workbook.
Exercise:

Take a comfortable position, relax and allow your body to become quiet and calm. Breathe deeply and make an inner affirmation: 'I am aware and I am ready to begin this journey'.

Imagine that you are in the country. It is spring. It is a very beautiful day and it is morning. The sun is shining, the sky is blue and there is a gentle breeze. You can feel that breeze on your face. You become aware of your surroundings. You can see flowers, meadows, trees. As you look off into the distance you can see hills and mountains.

On one of those hills you can see a temple. It is the temple

*This exercise was adapted from Piero Ferrucci, *What We May Be* (Turnstone Press, 1982).

of silence. It has a beautiful shiny exterior. You can see it far in the distance; look at its shape, its beautiful presence.

The temple of silence is on top of a hill and you start walking towards it. You can see that there is a path leading there. When you reach the path you begin to walk uphill. As you walk you become conscious of the sensation of the ground under your feet and the muscles in your legs. You are going to make the journey to the temple of silence. You will find everything you need along the way. As you walk you also become aware of nature around you.

You continue walking upwards, up the hill towards the temple of silence. You are almost there. You can see it getting closer and closer.

You are approaching the temple of silence now. The temple of silence is completely silent inside. No one has ever uttered a word there. You are in front of the temple and can touch its wooden doors. You can feel the texture of the wood on your hands. You know that once you enter the temple you will feel an atmosphere of timeless stillness and peace.

You push the door open and enter the temple of silence. You explore the temple and look around; as you do this, you increasingly feel the silence, a deep stillness. In the centre of the temple, there is a place to stand, within a ring of light. You walk into that space of light, where the rays converge, so that now you are surrounded by this beneficent light, pervaded by this luminous silence. Allow it to penetrate you, each part of you, each cell. You can breathe the silence, the stillness, the light. It is a very nourishing light. There is always more light—entering you, regenerating you, and always a magnificent silence.

Now you leave the temple through the doors you entered and go outside into the spring atmosphere. You again hear the birds singing, see the trees and nature surrounding you; and you can still feel the silence and light, the still peace pervading you. Slowly, little by little, you come back here to this room, bringing the silence with you. The temple of silence is in *you*.

When you're back, take some time to write in your psychological workbook about this experience.

PEAK EXPERIENCE MEDITATION

Recalling, remembering and reliving the most meaningful and

significant moments of life can nourish and regenerate us, inspire us and remind us of the meaning of life. In the everyday haste of life we tend to forget and lose touch with the beauty and poignancy it contains. This guided meditation has the purpose of reconnecting us with the depth of life. It also *reminds* us of the interconnectedness of ourselves with others.

Age: fourteen–adult
Time: 20 minutes
Equipment: Psychological workbook.
Exercise:

Sit comfortably, close your eyes, relax, and breathe deeply for a few moments. Recall some experience in the past when you had some kind of peak experience, some experience when you felt most fully you, a time you felt most real, most alive.

Go back as much as you can to what that was like. Re-experience it and relive it. Where were you? How old were you? Allow yourself as fully as possible to stay with this experience. Remember how it made you feel and think. Reconnect with the atmosphere and the feelings of this experience, the energy you felt. Get in touch with the quality of this event.

Imagine a few feet above you, above your head, the source from which that quality emanates, the source of that energy. Imagine that you begin to rise upward towards that source. As you draw closer to it, the energy becomes more intense. Now take a few deep breaths. As you inhale draw closer to the source, while as you exhale the energy fills up your body. Imagine this happening several times, breathing deeply.

Then gradually let yourself enter the source of this energy. Allow yourself to move toward its centre. Then let yourself expand, to become the source itself. Be aware of how you are that energy. You are the source.

That quality is in you. You are radiating it out around you. Look around, outward, and you'll see other sources of energy, of light—like other stars in a great galaxy. Make contact with them, live with them. Exchange energy with them. Be aware of how you all are part of other stars that are not shining fully yet, only dimly. As they receive light from you and other sources of light, and give light, they also become part of this great whole, always expanding and reaching out. In this way the energy from each source becomes available to all other sources.

Now gradually leave the collective source and focus on your own body, by imagining a cord of light that reaches from the source to the top of your head. Through that cord energy can flow from the source to you. Once more really be in touch with the quality of that energy and absorb it.

Find a word that can express that quality. Slowly come back into the room bringing that quality with you. When you are ready, write about your experience.

POSITIVE SELF-PORTRAITS

Too often a child or adolescent loses touch with his positive strengths and qualities and needs to be reminded of them. His self-image, in order to be realistic and true, needs to contain a clear awareness of these positive elements. Through the use of this exercise the participant is able to become aware of and make explicit his present positive qualities and/or those about to emerge.

Age: twelve–adult
Time: 40 minutes per participant
Exercise:
I would like you to take a few minutes to think about yourself. We are going to explore and get in touch with our positive qualities. Think about all the things you like about yourself. From little to big things, anything from the colour of your eyes to your ability to love your friends. When you are ready write those things down. Make a list of your positive qualities and aspects. Write down at least ten qualities or traits or aspects that you like about yourself.

Now form small groups. (The groups can be from six to ten.) Each person will have a turn to go through this process. When it is your turn, you give or assign to each person in your group one of your qualities. Tell them a little about what you are like with that particular quality. You are soon going to see your *positive self* manifested in physical form.

Each person who is 'mirroring' think for a moment about the quality or characteristic that has been assigned to you and that you will be expressing for your friend. Take a body posture or position that expresses this aspect. Make yourself into a symbolic statue or portrait of it. Use facial expression too.

Form a circle with the persons mirroring your qualities and place yourself in the centre. You can rearrange the statues if they aren't right. Get them exactly the way you want them to be to portray this part of you fully. (Educator: allow plenty of time for this to happen.)

When you are satisfied with all the statues, stand in the centre, looking slowly and attentively around the circle. Take them in and fully recognize and see your positive self there. This is you, a symbolic group portrait of you. This is what you are capable of being and becoming.

When you feel you have taken them in as a group, say to each individual: I am . . . (whatever the positive quality or characteristic is).

Each participant can go through the entire process. Alternatively, the exercise could be done over a period of days.

Processing the experience:
After completing the exercise, each person share with his group what it was like to see and experience his positive self right there in front of him. How willing was he to *own* these positive aspects? Is there any way to nourish these characteristics and to express them more?

THE TECHNIQUE OF RIGHT PROPORTIONS

Adolescence can be a time of great stress, of tremendous psychological movement from extremes of high and low, of up and down, while the young person is finding his identity and place in the world. It is easy to become overwhelmed and lost in the intensity of the moment and even to lose one's perspective. Learning to cultivate a right sense of proportions can be immensely valuable during this time and later in adulthood. It can alleviate a sense of isolation and provide a feeling of compassionate understanding, as well as an understanding that there is more than this or that intense feeling or thought or experience. This guided visualization has the purpose of facilitating a right sense of proportion and can be used regularly for doing so.*

Age: sixteen–adult

---

*This exercise was adapted from Piero Ferrucci, *What We May Be* (Turnstone Press, 1982).

Time: 15 minutes for the exercise
     15 minutes for processing the experience
Equipment: Psychological workbook.
Exercise:

Take a comfortable position, breathe deeply a few times, close your eyes, and turn your attention towards your inner world. Let your feelings calm down, let your thoughts slow down and become more peaceful and still.

Now imagine in detail the room in which you are sitting right now. See the chair you are sitting on, how you are dressed, and the people who are with you. See yourself and the group as a whole sitting here. Imagine that you can rise to the ceiling and take a look at the whole group beneath you.

Then you imagine moving higher up and away from the room, and form a clear picture of this building and the surrounding area.

You keep moving higher, and you can see this building becoming smaller as you move higher up. Now you see this whole area, houses, people, trees, parks, streets, bigger buildings, skyscrapers, and little cars moving in the streets.

Everything is getting slowly smaller as you move higher up. And while you see that, imagine how every being is the centre of his own world, with his own thoughts, hopes, needs, problems, projects and strivings. Observe the world beneath you, with all the people and living beings moving around, living their own lives. Imagine them in their own worlds, their homes, their surroundings.

Continue your ascent, and as your field of view expands you can see other towns and cities in the country as well as the landscapes in between. See the fields, the woods, the hills and the mountains. You can glimpse the whole of your country, the coastlines, the ocean around, as you move higher and see other countries. You see banks of clouds in between and then again vast spaces of other countries and eventually continents.

Now you have the whole planet Earth beneath you in your view. It is blue and white, slowly moving through space. You have moved so high that from this immense height you no longer see people or distinguish countries. You can still think of almost five billion people all breathing the same air, all living on the same planet—almost five billion hearts of the people of many different races are beating on that planet down there. Think about this for a few moments as you continue visualizing the Earth.

Now you continue to move further away from it and planet Earth becomes smaller and smaller as other planets come into your field of vision: Venus, bright and shiny, Mars with its intense red light, massive Jupiter, then Saturn with its rings. In fact you begin to see the whole solar system and you still move away. The earth is no longer visible, the sun is but a tiny twinkling point of light—among innumerable stars.

You have lost trace of who is what in all those tiny twinkling points of light, it is of no importance to you right now. Billions of stars are all around you, below, above, on all sides. There is no more down, no more up.

All of these billions of stars are contained in just one galaxy and this is one of an unknown number of galaxies in the universe. There are uncountable galaxies reaching out in every direction to immensity. At this point think of the infinity of time; there is no tomorrow here, and no yesterday, no future, no past, no pressure, no haste. Everything is scintillating peace and wonder here; everything is endless stillness.

When you feel inclined, you slowly move back through space. You move towards our galaxy. The sun becomes bigger again and you see the bluish colour of planet Earth enter your view again and come closer. You are again seeing the entire planet and moving towards it. You begin again to see the continents, the oceans, clouds. Now you see your country again. You descend lightly to your city, seeing houses and streets and people again. You see this street, this building. Now you see this room, this group and yourself sitting on your chair.

When you feel ready open your eyes and bring back with you this sense of expansion and timelessness. Take a few minutes to write about your experience.

Processing the experience:
Break into groups of four to six people and share your experiences. As you share, look at how this sense of perspective might influence the way you look at yourself and your life. Could this exercise be of any use to you in your life and how? What would be the appropriate time to do this exercise again? Are you willing to?

Chapter 8

EDUCATOR KNOW THYSELF

> It is the longing for personal unity, from which must be
> born a unity of mankind, which the educator should lay
> hold of and strengthen in his pupils. Faith in this unity
> and the will to achieve it is not a return to individualism,
> but a step beyond all the dividedness of individualism and
> collectivism. A great and full relation between man and
> man can only exist between unified and responsible
> persons.
>
> Martin Buber

Until this point we have given attention to the development
and unfoldment of the child or adolescent; but now, in a
sense, I am going to say 'Forget everything', none of this
matters unless we are prepared to look at ourselves—for we
teach what we are. Who *we* are is a further dimension which
cannot be excluded in a sincere consideration of any education
we may offer.

I begin this chapter with a note of compassion for the
immense task of the educator and the complexity of his task. It
demands that we maintain a balanced perspective of ourselves.
We are only human and I know that when faced with
responsibility for our young beings, and the sincerity which
this responsibility warrants, the task is frightening and our
resources will be stretched. *All* educators, parents and teachers
alike, from time to time feel overwhelmed by the task of
education. It is unavoidable; we become nervous, bored,
depressed, confused, angry, frustrated, and feel a distance
between us and the young. Sometimes we experience our

work as nothing but routine and our souls become lost in that routine. Despair is an all too frequent silent reaction. Although at heart we like our work, and have freely chosen our role, we may be plagued by a recurrent feeling of *something not quite working*. When we remember the optimism that accompanied our original choice to take on the task of educator, we may even begin to question whether or not we should be doing it at all.

Where did this feeling go that once inspired us to be and work with the young? Why does this paradoxical difficulty occur? Is the problem in the educational system, in the child, or in the educator himself? Changes made externally in mandates and policies, in systems and structures, in acquiring expensive new equipment, in higher salaries or smaller classes, will not bring relief to these difficulties. Our existential suffering in relation to the quality of our experience will not be alleviated by changes in forms.

The heart of the problem lies in the educator. There is something in us that needs to be touched, to be known and seen; that is what requires attention. Most likely we have postponed looking at this aspect of the problem—it is not comfortable to look, to probe, to be ruthlessly honest with ourselves. It requires courage: perhaps now is the time to address our own psychological state, which deeply influences our experience of educating and our expression as educators.

Even though children have a life and identity of their own which can be carefully examined, they sometimes act as a mirror for us—a pitiless mirror. If we are having difficulty with a child, or if a child is having difficulty with us, our natural reaction is to look at the child, to see the problem as lying within him. We must also look inside *ourselves* during these difficulties; look for *how* the child is mirroring us, *how we* are contributing to the problem. It is important that we are sufficiently in touch with our own unconscious in order to respect and understand the unconscious of the child.

Much of our world means but little to a child; our rules and regulations, our conscious morality, the words which we speak carry different meanings. In short, our overt behaviour is not the only reality a child perceives. The value of our contacts with a child depends upon both our inner reality and our outer behaviour. It is the sum total of our personality that we present to a child, that is perceived by his unconscious, and that he responds and reacts to. For example, have you entered a room where the atmosphere was charged with hostility and aggression although outwardly it was filled with polite and seemingly friendly people? A child is more sensitive, more vulnerable than you to these forces. He intuits the unspoken fears that we will not face, the unwelcome forces within ourselves and our repressed elements such as anger and aggression. Psychologically, whatever we refuse to face consciously remains unsolved but operative and a child is sensitive to it.

There is no truly effective solution but for the educator to turn his attention and searching inward towards himself. Often the child is a reminder of something which we wish to forget. The *problem* issues must be squarely faced and understood before we or the child can escape from their power.

We are all from time to time at the mercy of unknown forces within ourselves. If, for example, we feel dislike or resentment towards a child, we would do well to examine carefully the underlying motive of these feelings. It is possible that the child is somehow not complying with our own idiosyncratic view of how we would like things to be, or he represents something in our own unconscious which we fear to face. Rather than trying to forget or push aside such reactions, we need to examine our feelings with the greatest care and remain conscious of them when dealing with that child. Otherwise we relate to him through distorted perceptions.

How does this mechanism of a child mirroring our own unconscious life occur and what psychological dynamics are at work? To understand it we need to explore four dimensions: the nature of the unconscious of a child; the nature of our *own* unconscious with the hidden impact upon it of our *own* childhood; our *own* psychological defence mechanisms; and our own self-fulfilling expectations.

The Nature of the Child's Unconscious
A child's unconscious is deeply influenced by that of his parents and educators. He does not have a separate, independent unconscious himself until about eight years of age, nor a

separate identity until late adolescence. Until then he lives in a state of *emotional participation*, or identification, with significant people in his life. According to Jungian psychologist Frances Wickes, the ego of a developing person is still too unformed to set up barriers against the invasion of forces that move in the unconscious psyche of his educators. Even as his sense of self, of being separate from his surroundings, emerges, his unconscious is still held close in that identification. It is a psychological dependence. A result of this identification is that the disturbing forces which lie below the realm of conscious adult life are intuited by the unconscious of the child. They influence his behaviour, both in life-giving ways and destructive ways. This is especially true for younger children but throughout adolescence it remains a potent factor. Their influence is only broken as his ego attains a degree of conscious integration, which allows personal freedom of choice.

This certainly does not mean to say that a child is a total victim to his environment and educators. He is not merely a reflection or repetition of ourselves. Each child carries within himself the seed of his own individuality which is so important to cultivate. We often see in a family children, who are born of the same parents and brought up in the same environment, demonstrating very different behaviour and reactions. Yet in spite of these distinct differences, each child is, in his own unique way, greatly affected in his development and growth by his parents, his educators, and his environment.

Frances Wickes expresses it as follows:

> Many of us are so factually minded that we realise the importance of the objective experience, but are quite blind to the intensity and force of those intuitive experiences, which come when the child feels all that lies below the surface, though he is unable consciously to formulate these feelings even to himself. Children gather from us the atmosphere of all that we most carefully ignore in ourselves. If our unconscious goodness is founded on fear and repression, the atmosphere that we impart must be one of fear, restraint, or insincerity. If such destructive undercurrents are intuited by the child, he may resent the commands which seem reasonable; then resistance is raised and the spirit of rebellion against authority is

engendered. If, on the other hand, our attitude is a conscious acceptance of our own highest law, and a readiness to face the ever present forces within ourselves which may become manifest in evil as well as in good, then by that very attitude we stimulate a growth toward life and courage. The child then reacts to the motive which rules us, as well as to our spoken word.[1]

Self-knowledge As Educator

There is a reservoir of unconscious elements that govern and rule us, determining our behaviour and attitudes towards those we educate. We need to look at the hidden impact of our own past and childhood upon our adult life. It is when we can establish an authentic relationship with a child, which is free from attitudes and prejudices from our own past, that we can relate to him with fresh eyes, with clear perception *and* most effectively educate him.

It would be too extreme to say that we *are* our history; but it is commonly understood that our past experiences, especially in childhood, to a great extent influence how we behave as adults. This influence is multi-dimensional, often indirect, and all-pervasive. It affects our capacity to love and to be close to others, how we exert authority and assert ourselves, the manner in which we perceive the world, and our deepest attitudes and values. Lest we become puppets of the past, we can stop the chain of these unconscious mechanisms being passed down generation after generation, by becoming aware of them.

Like those we educate, we learn *how* to behave and relate to others from the models we had in childhood. We tend to repeat and perpetuate the same behaviour patterns. Parents who were not loved when they were children find it difficult to transmit love. They didn't have the opportunity to learn how, they have no models of what healthy love is like. Or if, for example, our self-image is poor and deprived, we will tend to perceive the world as critical and judgemental and our reactions will be defensive. If as children we were physically punished for misbehaviour, we will tend also towards physical punishment for our children. If we were taught that good children are quiet and well behaved—then we will assess the children we teach likewise. If we learned that to conform brought love—then we will love those children who conform.

If our childhood days were very structured and ordered and our own educators demonstrated a low tolerance for chaos—we, too, are likely to enforce order and structure, and even experience anxiety with the potential collapse of our tidy systems. If our childhood model for self-assertion was one of manipulation and covert demands—we too, may not be able to state directly what we want and assert our needs. The list is endless . . .

Let's explore in depth an example which is commonly experienced in all but the more saintly educators. It is unnecessary to point out how readily we can become angry with a child or adolescent, for various reasons, appropriate or inappropriate. Few of us have escaped feelings of wanting to throw a kid out of the window or physically control his behaviour. With so many children to cope with, teachers deserve considerable compassion for their natural anger and frustration with a child. How understandable it is to bang a hand on the desk and yell 'Shut up' to enforce discipline.

It is vital to know our own basic attitude towards anger and aggression. This attitude, too, is primarily formed through parental and social conditioning, both of which are generally repressive. Although anger is an honest feeling, our cultural attitude, simply stated, is that it's not nice to get angry. However it is what we *do* with our anger, and *how* we express it, if we do, that can cause trouble for both ourselves and our children.

If we are afraid of our own anger, we will reject and repress it. We may transmit the idea that the world is all sweet and nice but the atmosphere won't be authentic *or* we may lash out, directly or indirectly through our words, actions or attitude. We can be sure our anger will somehow be communicated, and those we communicate it to in turn learn that particular way of behaviour. Children often get double messages about anger. For example, they may experience the wrath of anger from adults through icy disapproval, but it is not acceptable for them to express their own anger in this or any other way. At an early age they often learn to suppress anger and even experience shame and guilt for feeling it.

In the perspective of psychosynthesis, aggression is a basic energy which is not just violence but a natural form of self-affirmation. We all need to assert ourselves; without doing so our self-esteem may be damaged. Obviously we cannot totally repress it or give it total free range. It is necessary to find a healthy balance, but if an educator is not able to find that balance for himself, how can he possibly help the child to find his own?

Anger and aggression is just one example of an area in which an educator needs to know himself. There are so many others. Not to know ourselves can have dire consequences. Portions of ourselves which are rejected and driven to the unconscious can, and inevitably do, break out, affecting our communications, our perceptions, and our actions. They influence how we perceive the world, what we can let it teach us, what we can take from it, what we can give to it.

Defence Mechanisms

If our perception of the young is distorted, our relationship with them will be distorted likewise. A defence mechanism, as conceived by Freud, is a perception adopted by our psyche in order to defend itself from something within us of which it is afraid. It is a psychological mechanism which preserves the stability of the personality, but it does so at the expense of distorting reality. It also has the function of lowering the level of anxiety, thereby helping us to maintain some stable level of functioning. As we will see, defence mechanisms are not necessarily only negative and harmful. The key is for us to be aware of our own defensive tendencies in order to limit their interference in our interactions with the young. The most common forms of defence mechanisms in interpersonal relationships fall into three categories: idealization, identification and projection.

Idealization

Idealization is the process of over-evaluating another person and putting him on a pedestal. What may come as a surprise to some is that children are often idealized by their parents and teachers. We have all known that perfect child—bright, well-behaved, creative, intelligent, attractive, bound to succeed with whatever he does. This child is a model of how we secretly feel *all* children should be. We praise that perfect child to the rest of the class or family and we use him as a yardstick by which to judge other children's behaviour. We seek out his contributions as we perceive them to be always right and we can count on him to fulfil our every expectation.

Little do we know what pressure we are putting on that poor child and how we are conditioning his inner life. For him, the price is high—the repression of any psychological element which does not correspond to our perception. He may become unable to allow himself to contemplate feelings or thoughts which he knows, consciously or unconsciously, do not fit our neatly labelled perceptual box. He may experience guilt and shame if his inhibitory reins fail and he acts spontaneously. He skilfully learns to pretend to be as we perceive him, but loses his sense of integrity and self-worth. I was one of those 'good' children, and the memory of the confusion this created remains vividly with me.

What drives an educator to idealize? If we are reluctant to recognize a dissatisfaction we have with ourselves, we find an *external* source for the security that we lack. We seek *outside* of ourselves that embodiment of perfection which we long for. We can escape the painful confrontation with our dissatisfaction and deep unconscious insecurities.

Identification

It is broadly accepted that it is appropriate for a child to identify with adult models, be they parents or teachers. Through this process of identification he learns and incorporates certain ways of being and certain qualities of behaviour. This is healthy, and a natural part of the journey towards individuality; and in most cases it ceases as the child finds his own identity. If the person with whom the child identifies is whole and well integrated, the child learns well the various expressions and characteristics of being human. He may also learn the various distortions and neuroses of his chosen models. Fortunately, identification is not usually limited to just one adult model, therefore the learning is fairly well rounded.

Why then is it inadvisable for an educator to identify with a child or adolescent? To identify with is to become more or less *one* with; when we identify with a child we invest ourselves in that person. We live through him, find our own identity and self-worth through him and depend on him for validation of both who we are and our value in life. We, too, are not limited to identifying with only one child but may identify with certain aspects or qualities of several children. What this essentially means is that when that child is not displaying well the aspect of him with which we have identified—he is letting us down, betraying us. The extent and intensity of our identification determines the extent and intensity of our dependency. Again this places a heavy burden upon the young person.

Identification usually covers a sense of inadequacy and unloveableness; it often masks that which we cannot face. We implicitly demand that our child be *all that we aren't* as well as what we wish we could have been. It is a vicarious fulfilment of our own frustrated *wish life,* which impedes the child from expressing and fulfilling his own needs. The classic example of this is the father who desperately wants his son to continue in *his* own career.

Projection
The last and perhaps biggest defence mechanism that we need to look at is projection. Projection means that we read into another person something that really exists in ourselves, or into a situation something we have found to be true in a previous occurrence or relationship.[2] It has the function of releasing anxiety, although we are seldom aware of what we are doing. We *export* elements of ourselves onto another person, and that other person may be our child or student. We tend to project onto others what we cannot *own,* accept or include as a part of ourself, such elements as we deem to be distasteful, unworthy and unacceptable. However, we may also project those positive qualities that are too great for us to contemplate.

Psychological elements that have once been conscious and then repressed tend to seek escape in the form of projection. These elements do not hide quietly in the basement—through the dynamic of projection we will find them in another person. Whenever we experience having a charged reaction to a young person, projection may be occurring. For example, if we are strongly irritated by a child, we may be seeing, in him, those things that we are unconsciously upset about within ourselves.

Unfortunately the recognition of projection is not easy. It

is not just a question of that which we don't like, or which we react to, in others being precisely what is in ourselves. In the usual style of the psyche the interpretation is less obvious and requires more probing and discrimination. Since the process of transformation is always at work in the unconscious, what emerges as projection may have a different form from what was repressed. It is often a revised version. Both the creator of a projection and its victim are unaware of the true nature of the projection; and the victim, of course, is not a totally blank screen either.

There will be an element of *truth* in the projection, that is to say that the individual will genuinely have some of whatever feelings are being projected. For example, if an educator is particularly indignant about a child's aggressive tendencies, it may be a mixture of his own aggression and the child's that he is perceiving. However, the degree to which the educator's reaction and response to this child's aggression is excessive, and out of proportion for the incident, will indicate the degree of projection.

The key to working with and re-owning any projection we suspect we have is to notice when our behaviour towards a young person is overly intense. If we experience having no freedom of choice regarding how we relate to a child, we can be sure that the lack of choice is telling us of some projected elements. I found myself strongly irritated not long ago with one of my students, and I could not summon up much patience with her. She always seemed to have a whining 'poor me' attitude and her basic statement was 'I can't do it'. Upon examining my irritation, I realized that there was a part of me, too, who felt this eternal 'I can't', but I was too busy to allow myself to pay attention to that part. I was confronting it in my student rather than myself.

I have also had to monitor myself carefully when confronted with those *ideal* students who perfectly adhere to my model of a *good learner*. I tend to see, in them, my own desire to please, to be a good person, to be a shining (but conforming) example of the charming, bright and overly positive learner. With these students I tend to over-react by giving them much of my attention, seeking their contribution in class, and reinforcing their overly positive behaviour. When this is occurring I leave little room for other students whose way is to learn by questioning, disagreeing, and fighting with the material in order to make it their own.

Female teachers have reported to me that they particularly find dominating, bully boy types especially irritating and they respond to these boys by being dominant and pushy themselves, whereas the more sensitive and caring boys receive more attention and are found more attractive. One educator told me of her habitual irritation with shy, babyish girls and that she positively seeks out the girls in the class who are independent and verbally articulate.

Another form of projection to which we may fall prey is altruistic surrender. This occurs when we attribute to our young our *own* needs and then try to satisfy those needs—in the other person rather than in ourselves. We seek to satisfy these unfulfilled needs vicariously and unconsciously through the other. This kind of projection is the result of being taught as children that our needs don't count, do not matter much, or even are bad—and that we must always put other people's needs before our own. The *self-sacrificing* educator who gives unendingly to his charges is an embodiment of altruistic surrender. The benefactor of such enduring giving can be left empty, smothered and unseen, and secretly resenting the tyranny of the positive. There is so often a mixture of truth and projection going on in these cases, that the best we can do is to discover our own underlying needs and fulfil them in conscious ways.

A similar form of projection, though generally less emotionally charged, is attributive projection. It is simply the tendency we all have to think or imagine that others are like ourselves. We assume that *how* we would like to be treated interpersonally, what we would want in a particular situation, and how we would feel if such and such happened, is equally true for those we educate. Hence we behave towards them in ways that we would want in such a situation. For example, we might be very gentle and loving with an especially shy child because that is how we would like our own shy aspects to be treated, when perhaps what is really best for that child is to be pushed more towards extroversion. The way in which we comfort and help a child with hurt feelings will tend to be how we would like our hurt feelings to be dealt with. Attributive projection flourishes at Christmas, for all of us, at times, buy the gifts for others that we ourselves would like to receive.

The most dangerous and extreme form of projection is projection of the *shadow*. According to Carl Jung, the shadow is the deepest, darkest, unresolved side of ourselves, which for most of us is totally unconscious. It is our blind rage, our prejudices, our destructive tendencies, and those unpleasant qualities, which are too negative for us to allow into our field of awareness. These projections are very powerful and cause other people, sometimes our young, to pay the price of our unresolved difficulties. Younger children's unconscious particularly fall prey to our projections of the shadow. This will indirectly influence their general sense of well-being and emerge symbolically through their fears and fantasies, their dreams and their irrational experience of reality.

Projection is directly felt by adolescents, who easily sense any strong negative feeling towards them. Jung said that we sometimes project the shadow in such a deep and potent way that we actually materialize it. An example of this is where all members of a family are very clean, nice and pure—except for one black sheep who is scapegoated and does *all* the bad things for the family. Teachers may find that one member of their class is *always* the one who does wrong, or is getting into trouble, seeming to personify all that we would define as destructive and unruly. Of course for us this particular child will increasingly embody the negative side of every young person and will have our opinion of him confirmed again and again . . . This is the converse projection to idealization.

The shadow is not always so overly negative; it may be less dramatic and simply contain those parts of ourselves that we have not integrated and fully experienced, such as our sexuality, our will to power, or our unresolved anger and aggression. In such cases we merely feel vaguely uncomfortable with the young person onto whom we were projecting; there is just something we don't quite like about him or we find ourselves avoiding authentic contact with him.

It requires great moral courage to meet our own shadow; it goes against that which is engrained in us. It is difficult to be willing to confront in ourselves what we do not like or accept in a young person but, as with all defence mechanisms, the cost is great if we do not. We will feel incomplete and sterile, and will most likely experience the world and others as being malevolent. In short, the world becomes a threatening place and we meet our shadow again and again *outside* of ourselves.

Self-fulfilling Prophecies

The concept of the self-fulfilling prophecy is an old idea and a simple one; it suggests that one's expectations for another person's behaviour can greatly affect their behaviour in the way that the prophecy is likely to come true. It means that one person's unfounded belief or conception about another comes to be realized.[3]

The first recorded self-fulfilling prophecy occurred in Greek mythology. A sculptor, Pygmalion, created an ivory statue of a beautiful maiden, and fell hopelessly in love with this statue. Her exquisite beauty touched him so deeply, symbolizing his own ideal, that he was beside himself. Venus, the goddess of love and beauty, was so moved by this that she gave the statue life in response to the sculptor's prayer. The self-fulfilling prophecy is sometimes known as the pygmalion effect. In George Bernard Shaw's famous play, *Pygmalion*, the relationship between Professor Higgins and Eliza Doolittle is a complex one and strangely similar to the relationship between educator and young person; it demonstrates both the positive and negative effects of expectations. In his outward role as her teacher Professor Higgins encouraged Eliza to learn certain language and behaviour, which would show that she was well born and bred. But deeply within he expected her to behave like a 'girl from the street' and thus it was difficult for her to do otherwise.

As Eliza Doolittle said to her admirer:

> You see the difference between a lady and a flowergirl is not *how* she behaves, but how she is treated. I shall always be a flowergirl to Professor Higgins, because he always treats me as a flowergirl, and always will; but I know I can become a lady to you, because you always treat me as a lady, and always will.[4]

Self-fulfilling prophecies have been clearly shown to influence the behaviour of others and much of the research on this subject has been done in the classroom. If a parent or teacher expects something from a child or adolescent, the result of this expectation is its transformation into reality. Our natural first reaction might be to protest and affirm that we want only the *best* and highest for our young. This I believe to be true; in our conscious awareness our wish is to educate and nurture our young. However, our motivation is not in question but our *unconscious*, subtle and negative expectations are . . . We do not deliberately set out to make a child fail, to be awkward, to have no artistic talents, to be a slow learner, to be shy or to show aggressive tendencies; but if we do have unconscious expectations, legitimate or not, the child will have difficulty not to comply with them. The younger the child, the more this occurs, as parents and teachers are the most influential people in a very young child's life. Research has even shown that expectations formed early on have a tendency to be passed from educator to educator, to follow a child through most of his educational life, and to accompany him into adulthood.

It has been found that middle-class children repeatedly do well in school while lower class, especially non-white, tend to do less well; and, interestingly, most teachers are middle class. They expect the children most like them to achieve, and unconsciously expect others not to. Recent educational studies in America have found that middle-class children often are not *actually* doing that well—but their teachers continue to perceive them as if they were. Factors that have been found to influence an educator's expectations unconsciously are: social class (most often imagining lower or working-class kids to do less well than middle or upper class), the actual name of the child, both Christian and surname, role perception according to nationality, and sexual roles. These are the areas where we tend to stereotype people.[5]

Paul Insel and Lenore Jacobson, educational psychologists, have defined a 'four factor' theory of the mediation of teacher expectations. This theory suggests that teachers favour pupils for whom they hold more favourable expectations by: (1) creating a warmer climate for them; (2) by giving them more differentiated feedback; (3) by teaching them more material; (4) by giving them greater opportunities to respond. Also, some communication of interpersonal expectations seems to occur along non-verbal channels, such as tone of voice, body movements and facial expressions. I will discuss this in more depth later.

Paul Kohn, sociologist, examines several studies on the relationship between teacher expectation and pupil performance, and recognized that teacher demands upon the quality of pupil work were determinants of that quality. His results further suggested that the attitude, evaluation or attraction of a teacher to a pupil, and the expression of these, can depend upon preconceived feelings about the pupil's ability.[6]

The point I am trying to make here is that educators need to trust their students' potential. I do not mean in an overly positive thinking way, but in the fabric of their being, in their deepest concept of what education means, and in their own implicit attitudes towards them. Here again, 'educator know thy self' is my plea. Our attitudes towards social classes, skin colour, sex, and our belief systems concerning the nature of human beings are especially important. These structures form the *ground* or the context through which we relate to the young and subtly colour both our perception and our way of responding. The impact of that context, of where we are coming from, is pervasive and greatly influences our behaviour.

To illustrate this point I give the example of a well-known and widely replicated research on self-fulfilling prophecy, done by Millard Blakley, of the University of Michigan in the United States. He was interested in finding out *how* prophecy was communicated from educator to student. To introduce the experimental expectation, some teachers were told that half of the students had exceptionally high achievement-potential, based on pre-test results obtained by the researcher, whereas the other half had typical or average potential. The information given to teachers was in fact based on a random selection of students, rather than on any actual test results, and was therefore a false prophecy.

The results were enlightening. The teachers behaved differently to the two categories of students in both verbal and non-verbal ways; they were more accepting, praising, warming and encouraging to the supposedly high-potential achievers, giving them more attention and support in their learning. The students from whom the teachers expected higher performance did actually perform significantly better than the others, even though pre-test results indicated no difference in learning potential.[7]

So how do these implicit, unspoken educator expectations get communicated to the child? It is not necessarily *what* we say, but *how* we say it—our tone of voice, subtle inflection, the way we hold our body as we communicate, and our facial expressions. The *truth* of our communication is often implicit. Non-verbal communication is not deliberate but tacit, silent and kinetic. Your body talks to me, and mine to you, independent of our words, and they make our unconscious thoughts transparent, perhaps to everyone but ourselves. There are many tiny subtle movements that show our positive and negative reactions. A child learns to read these small unconscious movements of his educator without even being aware of it himself. Their impact is as sure as if their message had been explicit.

Robert Koch, in his little-known article 'The Teacher and Non-verbal Communication', summarizes the main areas of body language in a useful way:

GESTURES: movements of the body, hands, feet, arms, legs, head and facial.
POSTURE: standing or sitting or changes in posture which occur during communication.
EYES: communicate with slight movements and expression.
SKIN: many signals are sent when the skin subtly changes colour and temperature.
PROXIMITY: generally we stay physically away from those we are least attracted to and are willing to be physically close to those we like. However, this may also communicate much about our own self-image and capacity for intimacy.
TACTILITY: when it is desired by the student and an authentic act by the teacher, it is a non-verbal action which is deep and lasting in effect.
VOICE: carries more than verbal content through tone, intonation, volume, pitch, hesitations, quivering and silence.
BREATHING: the speed and depth communicate feeling.[8]

The child's unconscious is sensitive to ours and it influences the formation of his self-image as well as behaviour. When we touch and talk to a child what does he really hear us say? He can invariably see through words that are covering the opposite feelings or language that is falsely used; he pays little attention to the surface *appearance* of our communication. He is an expert at intuiting authenticity. We cannot prevent our feelings toward a child being communicated through our body. For example, if we touch him in a loving way when we are really irritated—he will receive our irritation, not our love. What is more, we quickly lose his respect if our words don't coincide with our feelings.

This is our dilemma: we cannot communicate high, positive expectations of a child unless we truly have and feel them, and unless we believe in that child. Without our faith in him, our expectations will be lacking and he will know it. We can instead probe deeply within ourselves for these hidden truths and contextual prejudices and consciously create an I/thou relationship, to which I will refer in the following pages.

After Self-knowledge: Mastery

Self-knowledge, combined with consciously exploring our attitudes, expectations, prejudices, projections and behaviour patterns towards children and adolescents, can be a lengthy and sometimes seemingly unending task. We may discover unpleasant and disturbing truths about ourselves and feel that we lack the necessary qualities to be a truly effective educator. Fortunately, we are not necessarily victims to what we uncover nor are we limited to adapting to our limitations. We can become our own *master*, with the inner freedom to *choose* how we will be as educators. We can actively work to release the hold that our past has upon our present behaviour, thereby eliminating the obstacles to our expression of education. We can cultivate our strengths and expand upon our talents. Many of the techniques in this book, although supposedly for the young, are equally valid for you, the educator, and are included for your use too.

What is your intention? Are you able to make choices as an educator? Can you affirm yourself? Can you summon dynamic power and energy in your work? In short, where is your will and how do you use it as an educator? Without the will we do not feel potent in the task of educating. We will have difficulty in teaching students and in gaining their co-operation. With time and practice it is possible to find our centre, our Self—in the same way that I have suggested we facilitate young people. With self-identification we can find a place that is still and serene, that is inherently healthy, that knows and understands what's going on. And, most importantly, it is a place inside that has vision and can perceive both our own potential and that of those we educate.

In psychosynthesis we call that vision of potential an *ideal model*. It can be a living symbol of *what we may be* as educators, indeed what we may become as educators. The ideal model of oneself as the educator that one deeply *wills to be* is not an over-idealized unrealistic dream. It is based on a realistic perception of oneself, one's strengths, gifts and talents. We can cultivate and evoke qualities that are quietly brewing beneath the surface and that we never dared to dream of including in our self-image: qualities like love, joy, serenity, humour, compassion—those archetypal energies which we would like to be our gift to those we educate. We can consciously create a vision of ourselves and transform ourselves into that vision. Obviously an integral part of this process is the elimination of whatever in us is blocking this vision and preventing us from expressing it in our day-to-day educational work.

Ideals which are consciously held, cultivated, and actualized are of immense value and power; they energize us, bring us a sense of unity, can synthesize our various aspects and help us to feel whole. They can be like a star guiding us in the direction that we wish to move. Think for a moment what life and education would be like without ideals, hopes and the recognition of the greater workings of the evolutionary process. It would be a very sorry thing—opaque, dense, boring, blind, and leading to despair.

Without ideals there is no future, no life, no point in actually learning much of anything. How can an educator transmit and awaken students to ideals of beauty, of intelligence, of love, of creativity, of good will, unless he himself is enthusiastic about them, unless he himself is living them? The difference is between merely existing in an ordinary school or home routine and engaging the young in a process that inspires and charges them.

With the idea of living ideals, of having a higher vision of what we do, we are spilling over into the transpersonal domain, that realm of human experience which gives meaning and purpose, that we touch in moments of grace. Without this realm education is shallow, devoid of much more than rationality.

We may find that as educators we suffer from the *existential crisis*; the crisis of meaning where we have lost touch with the deeper motivation of our task. We might tend to experience educating as routine, shallow, and grey. Perhaps it has not always been that way; and we can remember the spark which ignited us to choose to have a child or to teach. Perhaps that spark was always unconscious for us and we need to uncover it. Our plight in the situation will not change until we begin to open up the transpersonal dimension and find the deeper meaning of our work, vision of what the true purpose is, the hidden meaning of the opportunity to touch and teach a young person.

On the other hand we may find that we have all of the above, the vision of how things could be, the ideals, the hopes for the job at hand, *and* that we are continually suffering from a state of dissatisfaction and frustration. Perhaps we *never* seem to meet this vision or actualize its beauty and we experience pain without that fulfilment. The gap between our vision of what could be and what actually is can be painful and will contribute to a sense of duality—the crisis of duality. Here we do not need to look to the transpersonal realm to find the meaning—we know it well; our task is to work on a personal level with whatever it is within us that prevents the manifestation of our vision. What are our weak points and how can we transform them? It is on the personal level, the level of integrating our personality and finding our 'I', that we need to work when we experience the crisis of duality.

I/Thou Relating

I have previously hinted that the *bottom line* of our becoming successful educators is the quality of our human relationship with those we educate, and I want to elaborate this point further. Martin Buber, a Jewish philosopher, coined the phrase I/Thou relationship. Buber claims that there are two types of relationships: the I/it relationship and the I/Thou relationship. In the I/it relationship we relate to others as objects: with expectations, anticipations, imaginings, with structures and borders, which reduces the other to an it or object.

The I/Thou relationship, on the other hand, is one without anticipation, without means and ulterior motives. It is an authentic relationship, from centre to centre. It reflects full respect and openness for the *being* of another person. It is a relationship which is always new, fresh, and filled with wonder. Buber believes that how the other becomes a *you* or a *Thou* is through the disintegration of expectation, greed, and boundaries—then the real encounter can occur. His message is that man becomes an 'I' only through a 'you', through the other. To Buber this can happen only through a moment of grace, whereas psychosynthesis fosters the conscious creation of I/Thou relating.

How? By creating a context in or from which to meet the young, a *ground* that holds the vision of this young person as a Self—a Being with whom we are privileged to be on a journey. We seek to acknowledge and honour this invisible reality; that the child is indeed a Self that has come into the world to evolve, to learn, and to grow. It is a truth to cherish, to know deeply. Children, especially young ones, are very much in touch with the ultimate unity. We see their longing to relate, their reaching for unity with their environment and with us. Little by little they abandon this *ground* of experience and, often with our help unfortunately, structures, boundaries and borders form. We could help them to maintain their essential knowing of the rightness of unity, of the *thou-ness* of the other. We could educate *ourselves* to see a child or adolescent from the context of the I/Thou relationship. If we reach out and relate to the young from this place, they will likewise respond from that place.

We can cultivate our vision of the potential of a child, the essential Beingness of each individual on a journey and in an unfolding process of becoming who they are. We can learn to trust the inherent gifts that each child has, and trust that differences are something to be appreciated. We can encourage him to be a Self by seeing the Self in him.

In conclusion then, the teaching is as high as the teacher. The most basic teaching is for us to get our *Self* together in human relationships. Unless we truly know ourselves, to use the exercises and techniques of this book with our students could merely be a diversion, a way to go unconscious, or a useless expenditure of time. Begin by using them on yourself. There is no set of exercises and techniques that will save you or completely transform you. They may stir something fresh and new into your consciousness, to help you to know yourself better, move you a few steps further in your own process, and give you some resources to proceed with on your own.

The paradox is that supposedly the work of this book is for us to do *with* children—but *the task of the educator and student is the same*. To accept the child and help him to learn what kind of person he is already—and to accept ourselves. To help him discover his aptitudes, his qualities, his potentials—and to discover our own. To 'bring the child out', to permit him to express and to act, to experiment, to make mistakes and to let himself be seen—and to give the same gift to ourselves. To remind him of the mystery and wonder of life—and to remember this ourselves.

It is not what we *do* with our young; it is who we are. No great teaching method will be enough if we ourselves are not 'at home'. We are all students and learners; the educator can educate only if he is willing to put himself into question as well. The answer does not lie in better classrooms, more equipment, team teaching, new tools and methods, although these things may help. It lies in you.

USEFUL INFORMATION

Various psychosynthesis centres and institutes are at present in the process of being born. Also, several individuals in various countries are doing psychosynthesis work independently of any institute or centre. The following list of available psychosynthesis sources is therefore incomplete and indicates only those centres and institutes which have been in existence for some time.

Asociación Argentina de Psicosintesis,
Juncal 2061 10-B,
Buenos Aires,
ARGENTINA
Berkshire Institute of Psychosynthesis,
Box 152,
Monterey,
MA 01245,
U.S.A.
Boston Center of Psychosynthesis,
Suite 400,
93 Union Street,
Newton Centre,
MA 02159,
U.S.A.

Centre de Psychosynthèse Enr./Psychosynthesis Center Reg.,
5840 McShane,
Montréal,
Québec,
H35 2G3,
CANADA
Centre Français de Psychosynthèse,
61 Rue de la Verrerie,
75004 Paris,
FRANCE
Centro Studi di Psicosintesi 'R. Assagioli'
Piazza Madonna 7,
50123 Florence,
ITALY
Greek Center for Psychosynthesis,
Evrou 4,
Athens 611,
GREECE
Kentucky Center for Psychosynthesis,
1226 Lakewood Drive,
Lexington,
KY 40502,
U.S.A.
Institute of Psychosynthesis,
1 Cambridge Gate,
Regents Park,
London NW1,
ENGLAND
Instituto di Psicosintesi,
Via San Domenico 16,
50133 Firenze,
ITALY
Instituto Español de Psicosintesis,
Hospital Neuropsiquietrico de la Virgen,
Carretera de Andalucia,
Granada,
SPAIN
Institute Mexicano de Psicosintesis A.C.,
Alfonso Reyes No. 147 Depto 4,
Colonia Condesa,
Condigo Postal 06 140,
MEXICO 11, DF

Psychosynthesis and Education Trust,
188-194 Old Street,
London EC1,
ENGLAND
Psychosynthesis Center/Highpoint Northwest,
23700 Edmonds Way,
Edmonds,
WA 98020,
U.S.A.
Psychosynthesis Training Center of High Point Foundation,
647 No. Madison Ave.,
Pasadena,
CA 91101,
U.S.A.
Stichting Psychosynthese,
Nederland,
Onstein 65,
1052 KK Amsterdam,
HOLLAND
Vermont Center for Psychosynthesis,
62 East Avenue,
Burlington,
VT 05401,
U.S.A.

NOTES

Chapter 1. What is Psychosynthesis?
1. R. Assagioli, 'Psychosynthesis and Education' (New York: Psychosynthesis Research Foundation), date unknown, p. 8.
2. R. Assagioli, *Psychosynthesis* (Turnstone Press, 1975), p. 17.

Chapter 2. The Techniques of The Work
1. G. Brown, *Human Teaching for Human Learning* (New York: Viking Press).
2. A. Huxley, 'Education on the Nonverbal Level', in R. Jones, *Contemporary Educational Psychology* (New York: Harper and Row, 1966).
3. R. de Mille, *Put Your Mother on the Ceiling* (New York: Viking Press, 1973), p. xii.
4. G. Hendricke, R. Wills, *The Centering Book* (New Jersey: Prentice-Hall Inc., 1975), p. 62.
5. R. de Mille, *op. cit.*, p. xii.
6. G. Castillo, *Left Handed Teaching* (New York: Praeger Publishers, 1974), p. 60.
7. R. Assagioli, *Psychosynthesis* (Turnstone Press, 1975), p. 144.
8. M. Crampton, 'The Use of Mental Imagery in Psychosynthesis' (New York: Psychosynthesis Research Foundation, Reprint No 12, 1969) p. 5.
9. R. Assagioli, *op. cit.*
10. R. Desoille, 'The Directed Daydream' (New York: Psychosynthesis Research Foundation, Issue No 18, 1966), p. 2.
11. R. Assagioli, 'Symbols of Transpersonal Experience' (New York: Psychosynthesis Research Foundation, Reprint No 11, 1969), p. 4.
12. R. Assagioli, 'Meditation', unpublished, (California: Psychosynthesis Institute).

13. R. de Mille, *op. cit.*, p. 16.
14. G. Hendricke, R. Wills, *op. cit.*, p. 169.
15. M. Crampton, 'The Use of Mental Imagery in Psychosynthesis' (New York: Psychosynthesis Research Foundation, Reprint No 12, 1969), p. 7.

Chapter 3. Growing Up Whole
1. P. Ferrucci, *What We May Be* (Turnstone Press, 1982), p. 96.
2. W. James, *Talks to Teachers on Psychology and to Students on Some of Life's Ideals* (Constable and Company Ltd, 1963), p. 75.
3. R. Assagioli, Meditation Group for the New Age, 'Education in the New Age', Third Course, Set II, p. 8.
4. W. James, *op. cit.*, p. 142.
5. G. Brown, 'I Have Things to Tell' (New York: Psychosynthesis Research Foundation, Reprint No 14, 1974), p. 7–9.

Chapter 4. Each of Us Is A Crowd
1. R. Assagioli, a course given at the Academia Fiberina, 1967.

Chapter 5. Our Hidden Strength
1. R. Assagioli, *Psychosynthesis* (Turnstone Press, 1975), p. 125.

Chapter 6. Adolescent Identity Struggles
1. R. Assagioli, 'For Parents Only' (unpublished paper).
2. R. Steiner, *Education as Art* (Steiner Press, 1972), p. 15.
3. R. Assagioli, *Psychosynthesis* (Turnstone Press, 1975), p. 111.

Chapter 7. Beyond What We Think We Are
1. E. Faar, 'The Philosopher Child Study, a Cross-Cultural Research Project', Psychosynthesis Institute, San Francisco, California.
2. R. Assagioli, Meditation Group for the New Age, 'Education in the New Age', Third Course, Set II, p. 8.
3. G. Weinstein, A. Alschuler, J. Evans, 'Toward a Theory of Self-Knowledge Development', Boston (unpublished paper).
4. P. Ferrucci, *What We May Be* (Turnstone Press, 1982), p. 130.
5. R. Assagioli, Meditation Group for the New Age, 'Education in the New Age', Third Course, Set II, p. 29.
6. R. Gerard, 'Psychosynthesis: a Psychotherapy for the Whole Man' (New York: Psychosynthesis Research Foundation, Issue No 4, 1964), p. 8.
7. R. Assagioli, *Psychosynthesis* (Turnstone Press, 1975), p. 100.
8. 'The Self and the Superconscious', Draft, Psychosynthesis Institute, San Francisco, California.

9. R. Assagioli, 'The Education of Gifted and Super-Gifted Children' (New York: Psychosynthesis Research Foundation, Issue No 8, 1960), p. 9.

Chapter 8: Educator Know Thyself

1. F. Wickes, *The Inner World of Childhood* (New York: Mentor and Plume Books, 1966), p. 39.
2. *Ibid.*
3. P. Insel, L. Jacobson, *What Do You Expect?* (California: Cummings, 1975), p. ix.
4. *Ibid.*, p. ix.
5. *Ibid.*, p. 103.
6. *Ibid.*, p. 40.
7. *Ibid.*, p. 221.
8. R. Koch, 'The Teacher and Nonverbal Communication', *Theory Into Practice*, Ohio State University, 1971.

INDEX

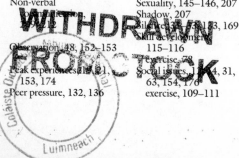